Constancy and Change in Architecture

Number One
Studies in Architecture and Culture

Constancy and Change in Architecture

Edited by Malcolm Quantrill and Bruce Webb

Texas A&M University Press, *College Station*

Library of Congress Cataloging-in-Publication Data

Constancy and change in architecture / edited by Malcolm Quantrill and
    Bruce Webb. — 1st ed.
        p.   cm. — (Studies in architecture and culture ; no. 1)
    Includes index.
    ISBN 0-89096-472-6
      1. Architecture and history.   2. Architecture and society.
I. Quantrill, Malcolm, 1931– . II. Webb, Bruce, 1941–
III. Series.
NA2543.H55C67   1991
720′.1 — dc20   90-23669
                                                 CIP

Contents

Illustrations

Preface

After the shock waves and controversies of Postmodernism and Deconstruction, alike in abnormal relationship to the past, the inaugural *Cubit* (CASA) symposium focused on a debate intended to reexamine architecture and explore the possibilities of "regrounding" it in more fertile soil. From this symposium comes the theme of the present volume, "Constancy and Change in Architecture."

To focus on constancy and change, it is necessary for us to understand our own *dwelling* in a particular time and place, and also to make connections with other times and places, yesterday and tomorrow. This involves traveling, in the mind, between our world and those other worlds. It also involves a sense of being in those other times and places, of developing an idea of what dwelling then and there was like, or will be. To do this we must make constructs; we have to reconstruct within ourselves those other frameworks of experience.

Our first resource in this process is our own dwelling, our own being in relation to things and places in the present time. In trying to understand the world about us—its form and nature—it is essential to see our own existence embedded in this present world. It is equally clear that we are not part of those other times and places: rather we are *apart* from them. We cannot actually dwell in the past, although we can diagnose its characteristics and construct its forms and patterns. perhaps what we need is a constructive partnership with the past.

Different times, places, and societies generate different patterns and forms; nevertheless in different times and places there are common themes and recurring forms. From the recurrence of these typical events, therefore, we can learn the typologies of form, since they provide evidence for the continuity of language and meaning in architecture. But in the nature of consciousness we can never confuse the past with the present, or other places with our own.

From this act of perception we see the nature of our present dilemma in architecture and the city. We know that our present being has its roots in the past; we understand how the forms and patterns of the past have given shape to our own world, our own thinking, and our doing. Yet we cannot relive the past with any more complicity than the future. We exist between those past structures and the ephemera of the future. Certainly, we can learn from the past, from the historical evolution of architecture and the city. The typological question generates valuable information about the nature of architectural form, its constants, and their variation. But we must be able to transform this knowledge and understanding about precedent in response to present and future needs. The piazza may have its charm, the café its delights, but how do these speak to the patterns of present-day Houston, or to the extreme cultural desolation of our suburbs?

This returns us to the very essence of dwelling, to our desire and capacity to root ourselves in things and places. While we cannot take steps backward and dwell in the past, are we capable of responses that will generate our dwelling in the present? Our generation's rewriting of history and our corresponding understanding of precedent, coupled with our accelerated interest in the future: all these shifts in knowledge, technology, and experience have transformed our concept of present time. We seem today to exist in a fluid state of being. Acutely aware of the historical process, we are not necessarily eager to learn from its lessons and principles. Indeed, both Postmodernism and Deconstruction have posited the abandonment of such systematic approaches and codified conduct. If Robert Venturi had not written *Complexity and Contradiction in Architecture,* it would have been necessary to invent such an author and text. Dwelling is the very antithesis of passing time, yet it is increasingly difficult to dwell — to root ourselves — in the present because of the technological acceleration of our clock. While looking over our shoulders at the precedents evolved in former ages, we are more and more aware of tomorrow.

By traveling in our minds between the present and other times and places, we seek to make connections, to build bridges of knowledge and cultural continuity. Our need to invent new structures means that we must learn from the body of knowledge at our disposal: it is necessary to know what preexists before we can invent variations and evolutionary forms to embody change. This is not to state a theoretical position. Rather, the recent insights of the neurosciences and cognitive sciences persuade us that the human animal learns and creates only by modifying what it already knows.

Education for the design of present and future structures requires models both of approach and of transformation. The identification of typologies is not enough: we must demonstrate their relevance to our own context. Education by reference to precedent, through the diagnosis of model forms, can introduce us to the basic notions of a framework for dwelling. Our capacity to dwell, however, stems from our own experience, from a human commitment to place in time.

Yet in our own time we discover that suburbs, which have human habitation as their core purpose, do not manifest the spirit of dwelling we observe in models from other times and places. Why is this so? Is it because the notion of dwelling, although we experience it as individuals, is manifested in most previous societies as a collective event, whereas suburbs resist any such collective forms and identity of association? Suburbs today represent not a sense of place or collective dwelling, but a number of unrelated private events. While our privacy is increasingly invaded, our sense of the significance of public place and space is also correspondingly diminished.

We can observe how in previous times and places there has been a *Zeitgeist,* or spirit of the age, clearly present in architectural form and detail. But can we detect a *Zeitgeist* today? We live in pluralistic, multivalent societies in which, in spite of theory, any set of models or values can seemingly be adapted to fit our time frame. Postmodernism in architecture has largely manifested itself as exercises in fashion, in the inversion and perversion of language. This could be viewed as the *Zeitgeist,* of course, in that it reflects the abandonment of clarity in favor of Venturi's "messy ambiguity." Also, there is more interest in answers than questions, as is demonstrated trivially by the proliferation of language games. Are we, in fact, running out of meaningful questions? Indeed, as the Deconstructionists would say, what could we possibly mean by "meaningful"?

Architecture is a lively art that continues to thrive and provoke us, in spite of repeated forecasts that it is in its final death throes. The role of buildings in the evolution of civilizations is complex and varied. Architecture is both background and foreground. We act out our lives against it, and we live and work in close proximity to its formal language. We inform architecture, and it informs us. And this exchange informs the lives that we live in and around buildings. The questions that we ask of architecture are therefore complex and varied. They change from one situation to another, and also from period to period. Yet the terms in which these questions can be asked are not themselves as varied throughout history. Although there are changes in scale and magnitude, and constructional techniques vary from period to period, and although the emphasis on one geometrical system rather than another differs from time to time, the planning and ordering of building forms and shapes obey a limited set of overall codes that recur again and again.

The language in which these forms are expressed is materially affected not only by means of construction, but also by the spatial intentions of designers. Baroque forms are distinctly different from those of the early Renaissance. Although they have the same geometrical sources, the difference is one of intent, of spatial reordering, that is not only constructed in the basic planning and building form but also emphasized in the details. The transformation from the uni-axial direction, the one-point perspective of the early Renaissance, to the multiple focus and centers of interest in the interlocking volumes of the Baroque, brings a new dynamic to the order of classical geometry. Indeed, the transformations from the work of Brunelleschi and Alberti to the profoundly different intentions of Palladio and Bernini offer convincing evidence of constancy and change within the framework of classical architecture.

In a similar way, we can understand how the work of Alvar Aalto from the mid-1930s progresses from the main line of international modernism, offering variations on basic modernist forms in search of a changing relationship between modern architecture and the cultural context in which it is being placed. Just as Renaissance architecture evolved new forms and solutions, partly in response to archaeological concerns with classical architecture and also to exploit new sources of order and planning in the realization of greater complexity in town and country, so Aalto's architecture began to demonstrate in modern terms that the constancy of new values was also subject to variation and change.

It is probably true to say that no modern historian has delved more deeply into the roots of constancy or reviewed the branches of change more thoroughly than Christian Norberg-Schulz. We therefore invited Professor Norberg-Schulz to be one of our principal contributors. Appropriately, as a reflection of the concerns I have tried to describe, he has entitled his paper "Order and Change in Architecture." This stress on order rather than constancy emphasizes the concept of an underlying structure, a constant set of values and concerns that allows and in fact even promotes and fosters variables and transformations. The Italian Renaissance did not generate a reproduction of classical architecture; it produced a transformation of classical ideas in response to another time that was a new period with quite different ideals and aims. In turn, Baroque architecture produced its own transformations, based on growing confidence in use of the classical vocabulary in spatial explorations and a rediscovered sense of the monumental.

In all these evolutions the element of time plays a crucial role. It is time that brings change, that modifies and reconstructs (or deconstructs) previous or existing order. We therefore invited Professor Karsten Harries of Yale University, whose field is philosophy but whose interest in architecture is renowned, to address the question of time in relation to our notion of constancy or order. His contribution, entitled "Time, Death, and Building," grapples with the problems of past order that are part of our knowledge and experience, and the dilemmas of our time and context in relating what we already know with our framework and program for action in the present. In Professor Harries's and Professor Norberg-Schulz's papers, and in their subsequent dialog, these difficulties are explored in relation to Martin Heidegger's philosophy, and our opportunities and the consequent provocation are revealed.

Kenneth Frampton chose as his topic "Rappel à l'Ordre: the Case for the Tectonic," concentrating our attention on the making of buildings, the putting together of architecture. This emphasis runs contrary, of course, to preoccupation with surface appearance. In making a case for the constructional aspects of the building art, Professor Frampton is concerned with the realization of the architectural idea through the section. The strength of spatial articulation comes through the basic tectonic form that molds and contains the architectural concept.

Yet our memory of structures is substantially affected by the play of surfaces and the images they frame or suggest. For example, Oleg Grabar confirms that medieval Islamic poetry interprets the surfaces of buildings rather than their structural core, implying that the originality and complexity of the royal monuments the poets praise is a property of their skin rather than their structure. This may well be the case, he suggests, because one discovers in a theme like the palace that it is the metaphysical memory and vision that ruled the physical reality. Not only in the palaces, but in the whole of Islamic architecture, this physical reality is delineated by the geometry and decoration of surfaces. Within the structural framework a whole web of pattern and color refers us to another, more ethereal world. A magician architect, Grabar says, could always change any stage into a new setting.

Perhaps this is Frampton's point, that the tectonic statement is the constant, which may be interpreted or reinterpreted by changes of detail and emphasis. Indeed, not just the language of architecture but the buildings themselves offer a framework for evolutionary interpretation. Within the forms the space is articulated, by structure, by light, and by the imagery of the enclosing, enveloping surfaces. In their discussion, Norberg-Schulz, Harries, and Frampton agree that these transient effects of building appearance illuminate the human relationship to change, time, and death.

These three essays and the discussion set the general framework of our enquiries, which is extended by the other essays included here. Together they attempt to bring the concerns of history, philosophy, and the design of buildings and cities into closer connection. From different viewpoints they focus on the relationship of time, place, and dwelling. Inclusion of Joseph Rykwert's essay, originally given as the 1988 Thomas Cubitt Lecture, and Grey Gowrie's essay, which is based on his 1990 Cubitt Lecture, offers a link between our present concerns and those to be addressed in the next volume, on emerging patterns in city and suburb. We hope this collection provides some helpful observations on our current dilemmas and the possibility of regrounding architecture with regard to both historic precedent and future prospect.

Richard Payne's photographs appearing in this volume dramatically illustrate the theme of continuity and change. They were made during the fall and winter of 1986 while he was in residence at the American Center in Paris. As an architectural photographer, Payne is best known for his photographs in two books on the work of Philip Johnson and John Burgee as well as *Historic Galveston, Landmarks of Texas Architecture*. He embarked on his European journey with a mission: to reenact Eugene Atget's famous nineteenth- and early twentieth-century photographs of Versailles and Paris. His procedure was to duplicate painstakingly the exact angle of view, vantage point, time of day, and quality of light that Atget had recorded, so that each pair of photographs would reveal elements of constancy and change in the scene over the intervening years.

Payne also turned his camera on other scenes which caught his eye in travels through France, England, Greece, and Italy, capturing a sense of places, both familiar and strange, existing in time where the visual evidence of the life and works of different ages are brought into an instant of poetic conjunction.

The photographs present vivid evidence of how time and locale collude, sealing together the ideas of constancy and change into a single concept, which may be the exact equivalent of the concept of place. The photographs seem to see instants where time is drifting through a scene, sifting over it like a restless wing, seeing what will blow away, what will remain, what has always been.

Our inquiry into the topic "Constancy and Change in Architecture" was intended to investigate some idea which lies behind, beyond, within—not on the surface of—architecture. It is an idea concerned less with material permanences than with the immaterial existence of architecture as the embodiment of powerful impulses which flex first in the human psyche as poetic constructs of dwelling: in Frances Yates's terms, "the immaterial existence in the mind of the architect before it is built and also [the] many immaterial existences in the memory of those who have seen it." An awareness of this immaterial existence is not the usual subject for architectural photographs which seek to use the photograph as an isolated specimen, arranged to be a kind of verification of the text. In matters of description the picture is always given primacy over the text, a position it achieves through a pretense of objectivity. This is a remarkable thing, since the photograph itself is extraordinary reality. Despite the presumption of veracity that gives photographs their authority, the work that photographers do, Susan Sontag writes, "is in no way a generic exception to the shady commerce between art and truth." This "shady commerce" is particularly evident when the image recorded by the photographer is misunderstood to be a picture of the thing itself rather than some idea about it.

Norman Mailer in his story "The Notebook" tells of an argument between a writer and his girlfriend. As they argue, he jots down in his notebook an idea for a story. It is a story about a writer who gets an idea for a story while he is arguing with his girlfriend. In this infinite regression of self-referencing storyteller and stories, there is a discovery of an empty infinity similar to the paradox of a mirror facing a mirror, creating reflection extending to infinity. Payne has been able to break this vicious cycling between text and image by shifting his mirror just enough for the reflections not to be equivalent and self-referencing.

Place does not dwell in the eternal present. It wanders.

Malcolm Quantrill
Bruce Webb

Norberg-Schulz, Arkitekthogskolen il Oslo, Norway; Marja-Riitta Norri, Museum of Finnish Architecture, Helsinki; Timo Penttilä, Siena, Italy; Alberto Perez-Gomez, McGill University; Ivor Richards, University of Wales; Herman Saatkamp, Texas A&M University; Norman Sherry, Trinity University, San Antonio; Thomas Thiis-Evensen, Arkitekthogskolen i Oslo, Norway; Malcolm Quantrill, Texas A&M University (editor-in-chief); and Bruce Webb, University of Houston (co-editor).

Finally, we owe a debt of gratitude to David Woodcock, who in his capacity as a member of the Advisory Board of Texas A&M Press was also instrumental in advancing the cause of the Studies in Architecture and Culture.

Rappel à l'Ordre: The Case for the Tectonic

Kenneth Frampton

The tectonic reemerges as a critical category today because of the current tendency to reduce architecture to scenography. This reaction arises out of the universal triumph of Robert Venturi's decorated shed, that is to say from a prevalent tendency today to treat architecture as though it were a giant commodity. Among the seductions of the scenographic is the fact that the results are eminently amortizable, with all the deleterious consequences that this attitude entails for the future of the environment. This degenerative prospect is accompanied by the general dissolution of stable references in today's world. With the singular exception of the field of techno-science, the precepts governing almost every discourse seem suddenly to have become extremely tenuous. Much of this was surely foreseen half a century ago by Hans Sedlmayr, when he wrote in 1941:

> The shift of man's spiritual center of gravity towards the inorganic, his feeling of his way into the inorganic world may indeed legitimately be called a cosmic disturbance. It is first of all a disturbance in the microcosm of man, who now begins to show a one-sided development of his faculties. . . . At the other extreme there is a disturbance of macrocosmic relationships, a result of the especial favour and protection which the inorganic now enjoys— almost always at the expense, not to say ruin, of the organic. The raping and destruction of the earth, the nourisher of man, is an obvious example and one which in its turn reflects the distortion of the human microcosm for the spiritual side of man pays just that kind of price and is subject to a similar process of ruin, and the end is that man having denied the reality of all higher forms of being, becomes utterly rooted in the inorganic sphere.[1]

Faced with this prospect of spiritual and material ruin, we are compelled to turn to certain rearguard positions, in order to recover a basis from which to resist. Today we find ourselves in a position similar to that of the critic Clement Greenberg who, in his 1965 essay "Modernist Painting," attempted to reformulate a ground for painting in the following terms:

> Having been denied by the Enlightenment of all tasks they could take seriously, they [the arts] looked as though they were going to be assimilated to entertainment pure and simple, and entertainment itself looked as though it

were going to be assimilated, like religion, to therapy. The arts could save themselves from this levelling down only by demonstrating that the kind of experience they provided was valuable in its own right, and not to be obtained from any other kind of activity.[2]

If one poses the question of what might be comparable ground for architecture, then one must turn to a similar material base, namely that architecture must of necessity be embodied in structural and constructional form. My present stress on the latter rather than on spatial enclosure stems from an attempt to evaluate twentieth-century architecture in terms of continuity and inflection rather than in terms of originality as an end in itself.

In his 1980 essay, "Avant-Garde and Continuity," the Italian architect Giorgio Grassi commented on the impact of avant-gardist art on architecture:

> As far as the vanguards of Modern Movement are concerned, they invariably follow in the wake of the figurative arts. . . . Cubism, Suprematism, Neoplasticism, etc., are all forms of investigation born and developed in the realm of the figurative arts, and only as a second thought carried over into architecture as well. It is actually pathetic to see the architects of that "heroic" period and the best among them, trying with difficulty to accommodate themselves to these "isms"; experimenting in a perplexed manner because of their fascination with the new doctrines, measuring them only later to realize their ineffectuality.[3]

While it is disconcerting to have to recognize that there may well be a fundamental break between the figurative origins of abstract art and the constructional basis of tectonic form, this recognition is a convenient position from which to challenge spatial invention as an end in itself—a pressure to which the architecture of this century has been unduly subject. Rather than support the current reiteration of avant-gardist tropes, or enter into the cause of historical pastiche, or reduce architecture to little more than the large scale sculptural gesture, these structures having an arbitrary dimension to the degree that they are based neither in structure nor in construction, we may return instead to the structural unit as the irreducible essence of architectural form.

Needless to say, we are not alluding here to the mechanical revelation of construction, but rather to a potentially poetic manifestation of structure in the original Greek sense of *poesis* as an act of making and revealing. While I am well aware of the conservative connotation that may be ascribed to Grassi's polemic, his critical perceptions cause us to question the very idea of the new, in a moment that oscillates between the cultivation of a resistant culture and a descent into value-free estheticism. Perhaps the most balanced assessment of Grassi has been made by the Catalan critic, Ignasi Sola Morales, when he wrote:

> Architecture is posited as a craft, that is to say, as the practical application

of established knowledge through rules of the different levels of intervention. Thus, no notion of architecture as problem-solving, as innovation, or as invention *ex novo,* is present in Grassi's thinking, since he is interested in showing the permanent, the evident, and the given character of knowledge in the making of architecture.

. . . The work of Grassi is born of a reflection upon the essential resources of discipline, and it focuses upon specific media which determine not only aesthetic choices but also the ethical content of its cultural contribution. Through these channels of ethical and political will, the concern of the Enlightenment . . . becomes enriched in its most critical tone. It is not solely the superiority of reason and the analysis of form which are indicated, but rather, the critical role (in the Kantian sense of the term) that is, the judgement of values, the very lack of which is felt in society today. . . . In the sense that his architecture is a meta-language, a reflection on the contradictions of its own practice, his work acquires the appeal of something that is both frustrating and noble.[4]

The dictionary definition of the term *tectonic* to mean "pertaining to building or construction in general; constructional, constructive used especially in reference to architecture and the kindred arts," is a little reductive compared to our present intention: tectonics comprises not only the structural component in itself but also the amplification of structure as presence in form in relation to the total assembly. From its conscious emergence in the middle of the nineteenth century with the writings of Karl Bottischer and Gottfried Semper, the term tectonic has not only alluded to structural and material probity but also to a poetics of construction, as this may be practiced in architecture and the related arts.

The beginnings of the modern, dating back at least two centuries, and the much more recent advent of the Postmodern are inextricably bound up with the ambiguities introduced into western architecture by the primacy given to the scenographic in the evolution of the bourgeois world. However, building remains essentially tectonic rather than scenographic in character, and it may well be argued that it is an act of construction first, rather than a discourse predicated on surface, volume, and plan, to cite the "Three Reminders to Architects," as these appear in Le Corbusier's *Vers une architecture* of 1923. Thus one may assert that building is *ontological* rather than *representational* in character and that built form is a presence rather than something standing for an absence. Following Martin Heidegger's terminology we may elect to think of it as a "thing" rather than a "sign."

I have chosen to engage this theme because I believe it is necessary for architects to reposition themselves, given that the predominant tendency today is to reduce all architectural production expression to the level of a commodity. Inasmuch as such resistance has little chance of being widely accepted, the "rearguard" character of this position is inevitable and, in the last analysis, possibly more realistic than the dubious assumption that it is possible to continue with the perpetuation of avant-gardism. Despite its concern for structure, an emphasis on tectonic form does not necessarily favor either Constructivism or Deconstructivism. In this sense one may claim that it is astylistic. Of the utmost import, however, is the fact that it does not seek to derive its legitimacy from either science, literature, or art.

Greek in origin, the term tectonic derives from *tekton,* signifying carpenter or builder. This in turn stems from the Sanskrit *taksan,* referring to the craft of carpentry and to the use of the ax. Remnants of a similar term can also be found in Vedic, where again it refers to carpentry. In Greek it appears in Homer, where it alludes to carpentry and to the art of construction in general. The poetic connotation of the term first appears in Sappho where the *tekton,* the carpenter, assumes the role of the poet. This meaning undergoes further evolution as the term passes from being something specific and physical, such as carpentry, to the more generic notion of construction and later to becoming an aspect of poetry. In Aristophanes we find that the idea is even associated with machination and the creation of false things. This etymological evolution would suggest a gradual passage from the ontological to the representational. Finally, the Latin term *architectus* derives from the Greek *archi* (a person of authority) and *tekton* (a craftsman or builder).

The earliest use of the term tectonic in English dates from 1656, when it appeared in a glossary meaning "belonging to building"—almost a century after the first English use of the word architect in 1563. In 1850 the German oriental scholar K. O. Muller was to define the term rather widely as "a series of arts which form and perfect vessels, implements, dwelling and places of assembly."[5] The term is first elaborated in a modern sense in Karl Bottischer's *The Tectonic of the Hellenes* of 1844–52 and Gottfried Semper's essay *The Four Elements of Architecture* of 1851.[6] It is further developed in Semper's unfinished study, *Style in the Technical and Tectonic Arts or Practical Aesthetic,* published between 1860 and 1863.[7]

The tectonic cannot be divorced from the technological, and it is this which gives a certain ambivalence to the term. In this regard it is possible to identify three distinct building conditions: (1) the technological object that arises out of meeting a given need directly, (2) the scenographic object that is used to allude to an absent element, and (3) the tectonic object that appears in both an ontological and a representational mode. The first of these tectonic modes involves a constructional element that is shaped so as to emphasize its objective presence and its mythic status. This is the tectonic as it appears in Bottischer's interpretation of the Doric column. The second mode involves the representation of an equally mythical tectonic element which is present as technique but hidden as form. These two modes can be seen as paralleling, to some degree, the distinction that Semper draws between the "structural-technical" and the "structural-symbolic."

Aside from these distinctions. Semper was to divide built form into two separate material procedures: the tectonics of the frame in which the members of varying lengths are conjoined to encompass a spatial field; and the *stereotomics* of the compressive mass which, while it may embody space, is constructed through the piling up of identical units—the term stereotomics coming from the Greek terms for solid, *stereos,* and for cutting, *-tomia.* In the first case, the most common material throughout history has been wood or its tensile equivalents such as bamboo, wattle, and basketwork. In the second case, one of the ubiquitous materials has been brick or the compressive equivalent of brick such as rock, stone, or rammed earth and later, reinforced concrete.

There have been significant exceptions to this division, particularly where, in the interest of permanence, stone has been cut, dressed, and erected in such a way as to assume the form and function of a frame. While these facts are so familiar that they hardly need repetition, we tend to be unaware of the ontological consequences of these differences: that is to say, of the way in which the framework tends towards the aerial and dematerialization, whereas mass tends towards the telluric; one presupposes light, the other darkness. These gravitational opposites, the immateriality of the frame and the materiality of the mass, symbolize the cosmological opposites to which they aspire, sky and earth. Despite our secularized technoscientific age, these contingencies remain as the experiential limits of our lives. It is arguable that the practice of architecture is impoverished to the extent that we fail to recognize these transcultural values and the way in which they are intrinsically latent in all structural form. Indeed, these forms may serve to remind us, after Heidegger, that inanimate objects may also evoke participate in Being, and that through this analogy the body of a building may be perceived as though it were literally a physique. This brings us back to Semper's privileging of the joint as the primordial element, the fundamental nexus around which building comes into being—comes to be articulated as a presence in itself.

Semper's emphasis on the joint implies that fundamental syntactical transitions are expressed as one passes from the stereotomic base to the tectonic frame, and that such transitions constitute the very essence of architecture. Moreover they are the dominant constituents whereby one culture differentiates itself from the next. There is a spiritual value residing in the particularities of a given joint that guarantees, so to speak, the "thingness" of the constructed object, so much so that it becomes a point of ontological condensation rather than merely a connection.

The first volume of the fourth edition of Karl Bottischer's *The Tectonic of the Hellenes* appeared in 1843, two years after Karl Friedrich Schinkel's death in 1841. This publication was followed by three subsequent volumes which appeared at intervals over the next decade, the last in 1852, the year in which Semper published his essay *The Four Elements of Architecture.* Bottischer elaborated the concept of the tectonic in a number of significant ways. At one level he envisaged construction as an appropriate interlocking of two constructional elements. Simultaneously articulated and integrated, these conjunctions were seen as body forms, as *Körperbildungen* that not only guaranteed the material finish of a building, but also enabled this form to acquire symbolic meaning. At another level, Bottischer distinguished between the *Kernform* or structural nucleus and the *Kunstform* or decorative cladding, the latter having the purpose of representing and symbolizing the cultural institutional status of the former. According to Bottischer, this shell or revetment had to be capable of revealing the inner essence of the tectonic. At the same time Bottischer insisted that one should always try to distinguish between the indispensable structural form and its enrichment, irrespective of whether the latter is merely the shaping of the technical elements as in the case of the Doric column or the cladding of its basic form with revetment. Semper would later adapt this notion of *Kunstform* to the idea of *Bekleidung,* the concept of literally "dressing" the fabric of a structure.

Bottischer was greatly influenced by the view of the philosopher Josef von Schelling that architecture transcends the mere pragmatism of building by virtue of assuming symbolic significance. For Schelling and Bottischer alike, the inorganic had no symbolic meaning, and hence structural form could only acquire symbolic value by virtue of its capacity to engender analogies between tectonic and organic form. However, any kind of direct imitation of natural form was to be avoided since both men held the view that architecture was an imitative art only in so far as it imitated itself. This view tends to corroborate Grassi's contention that architecture has always been distanced from the figurative arts, even if its form can be seen as paralleling nature. In this capacity architecture simultaneously serves both as a metaphor of and as a foil to the organic. In tracing this thought retrospectively, one may cite Semper's "Theory of Formal Beauty" of 1856, in which he no longer grouped architecture with painting and sculpture as a plastic art, but with dance and music as a cosmic art; that is to say, he sees it as an ontological world-making art rather than as a static representational form.[8] Semper regarded such arts as world-making not only because they were symbolic but also because they embodied man's underlying erotic urge to strike a beat, string a necklace, or weave a pattern, and thus to decorate according to a rhythmic law.

Semper's *Four Elements of Architecture* of 1852 brings the discussion full circle inasmuch as Semper added a specific anthropological dimension to the idea of tectonic form. Semper's theoretical schema constitutes a fundamental break with the fifteenth-century humanist formula of *utilitas, firmitas, venustas* borrowed from Vitruvius, that had first served as the intentional triad of Roman architecture and then as the underpinning of post-Vitruvian architectural theory. Semper's radical reformulation stemmed from his seeing a model of a Caribbean hut in the Crystal Palace exhibition staged in London in 1851. The empirical reality of this simple shelter caused Semper to reject the primordial model of the primitive hut, which constituted the point of departure and indeed the frontispiece of Laugier's *Essai sur l'architecture* published in 1753. Laugier employed this hypothetical paradigm as a way of legitimizing the pedimented temple front form in Neoclassical architecture. Semper's *Four Elements* challenged this assumption and asserted instead a cultural construct comprising (1) a hearth, (2) an earthwork, (3) a framework and a roof, and (4) an enclosing membrane.

While Semper's elemental model repudiated Neoclassical authority, it nonetheless gave primacy to the frame over the load-bearing mass. At the same time, Semper's four-part thesis recognized the primary importance of the earthwork, that is to say, of a telluric mass that serves in one way or another to anchor the frame or the masonry wall in the sense of *Das Mauer,* in the site.

This marking, shaping, and preparing of ground by means of an earthwork had a number of theoretical ramifications. On one hand, it isolated the enclosing membrane as a differentiating act so that the *textural* could be literally identified with the protolinguistic art of textile production that Semper regarded as the basis of all civilization. On the other hand, as Rosemary Bletter has pointed out, by stressing the earthwork as the fundamental basic form, Semper gave symbolic import to a nonspatial element, namely, the hearth that was invariably an inseparable part of the earthwork. The phrase *breaking ground* and the metaphorical use of the word *foundation* are both obviously related to the primacy of the earthwork and, by implication, to the symbolic importance of the hearth.

In more ways than one Semper grounded his theory of architecture in a phenomenal element having strong social and spiritual connotations. For Semper the hearth's origin was linked to that of the altar, and as such it was the spiritual nexus of architectural form. The hearth bears within itself significant connotations in this regard. It derives from the Latin verb *aedisficare,* which in its turn is the origin of the English word edifice, meaning literally "to make a hearth." The latent institutional connotations of both hearth and edifice are further suggested by the verb *to edify,* which means to educate, strengthen, and instruct.

Over the last century and a half, the field of cultural anthropology has afforded ample corroboration of Semper's basic thesis. Perhaps nowhere has this been more the case than in Pierre Bourdieu's analysis of the Berber house, first published as "The Berber House or the World Reversed" in 1969.[9]

While this analysis corroborates Semper's quadripartite theory, it also embodies a remarkable magic-mythical elaboration of its constituent parts. In this peculiarly dense example we will see how the typical Berber house constitutes a cosmos itself and the way in which this tectonic order is inseparable from the language and mores of the society and from the larger articulation of the society beyond the confines of the house.

The Berber house, unlike the nomadic tent, is largely a stereotomic work comprising an earthwork/hearth that is extended upwards as four mud-brick walls that double as the support for the wooden tectonic framework of the roof and attic. According to extensive anthropological sources cited by Bourdieu, the Berber house is homologically coded so as to create a dyadic and reversible cosmos, in which a whole set of interwoven polarities establish and sustain the ethical, sexual, and linguistic order of the society. The way in which these oppositions acquire their initial status, so to speak, from the earthwork and the roof enriches the potential significance of Semper's four elements.

The differentiation of the respective floor levels and the different finishes adopted divide the house into a homologous system, wherein the lower, flag-stoned floor towards the south is opposed to the higher, polished cow-dung floor to the north. The former, occupied almost exclusively by cattle, is associated with dampness, darkness, fertility, and death, with the wetness of defecation draining into the ground through the open joints in the flag-stone floor. Conversely, the larger two-thirds of the total floor area, set some fifty centimeters above the lower third, is associated with dryness, light, fire, food, and life. Needless to say, the hearth set into the earthen floor is located in this area, close to the external northern wall of the dwelling and thus as far as possible from the dampness of the southern end.

Finally it needs to be noted that the basic framework of the attic and roof is structured about a central column, known as a *thigejdith,* identified with the male member, and that this in turn supports the *aslar* or principal female cross-beam upon which all the other rafters rest. The central column is positioned off center on one axis. Its point of bearing coincides with the line of division between the upper two-thirds and the lower third of the earthwork.

Influenced by linguistic and anthropological insights of his age, Semper was preoccupied with the etymology of building. Thus he distinguished the massiveness of a fortified stone wall as indicated by the term *Das Mauer* from light frame and infill, such as the wattle and daub of medival domestic building, for which the term *Die Wand* is reserved in German. This fundamental distinction has been nowhere more graphically expressed than in Karl Gurber's reconstruction of a medieval German town (fig. 1.1).[10] While we have only one word for *wall* in English, the term *Die Wand* in German is related to the word for dress, *Gewand,* and to the term *Winden,* which means to embroider. In accordance with the primacy accorded textiles, Semper maintained that the earliest basic structural artifact was the knot, which predominates in nomadic building form, especially in the Bedouin tent and its textile interior. We may return here in passing to Bourdieu's field analysis of the Bedouin house wherein the loom is identified as the female place of honor and the sun of the interior. The primacy of the knot entails further etymological connotations of which Semper was fully aware, above all the connection between *knot* and *joint,* the former in German being *die Knoten* and the lat-

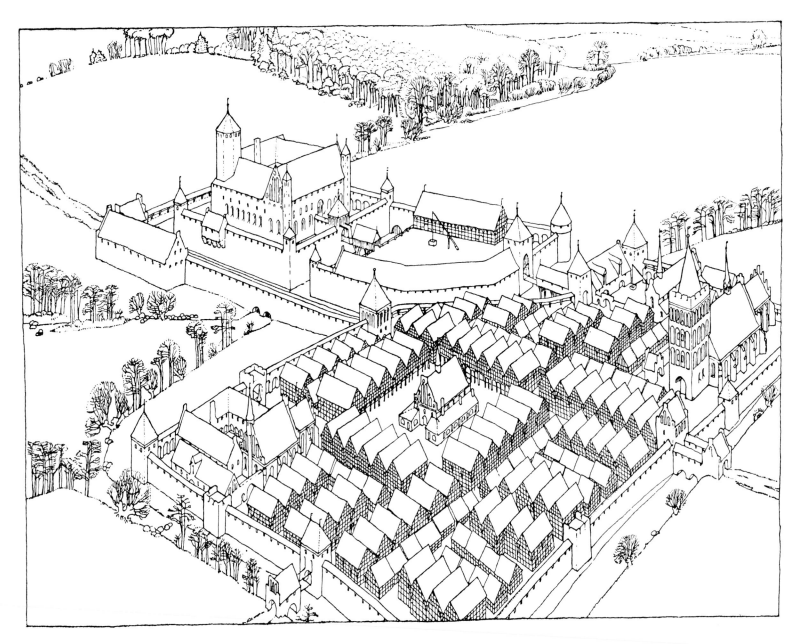

Fig. 1.1. Ideal view of a medieval town from *Die Gestalt der deutschen Stadt* by Karl Gruber, 1937. The didactic difference between a massive forti- fied *Mauer* and a lightweight woven *Wand* is indicated very clearly in this drawing.

ter being *die Naht.* In modern German both words are related to *die Verbindung,* which may be literally translated as "the binding." All this evidence tends to support Semper's contention that the ultimate constituent of the art of building was the joint.

The primacy that Semper accorded to the knot seems to be supported by Günther Nitschke's research into Japanese binding and unbinding rituals as set forth in his seminal essay *Shi-Me* of 1979. In Shinto culture these prototectonic binding rituals constitute the intrinsic symbolic (sacred) content of agrarian renewal and land-marking rites. Once again they point to that close association between building, dwelling, cultivating, and being, remarked on by Martin Heidegger in his essay "Building Dwelling Thinking" of 1954.

Semper's distinction between tectonic and stereotomic returns us to theoretical arguments recently advanced by the Italian architect Vittorio Gregotti, who proposes that the marking of ground, rather than the primitive hut, is the primordial tectonic act. In his 1983 address to the New York Architectural League, Gregotti stated:

> The worst enemy of modern architecture is the idea of space considered solely in terms of its economic and technical exigencies indifferent to the idea of the site.
>
> The built environment that surrounds us is, we believe, the physical representation of its history, and the way in which it has accumulated different levels of meaning to form the specific quality of the site, *not* just for what it appears to be, in perceptual terms, but for what it is in structural terms.
>
> Geography is the description of how the signs of history have become forms, therefore the architectural project is charged with the task of revealing the essence of the geo-environmental context through the transformation of form. The environment is therefore not a system in which to dissolve architecture. On the contrary, it is the most important material from which to develop the project.
>
> Indeed, through the concept of the site and the principle of settlement, the environment becomes the essence of architectural production. From this vantage point, new principles and methods can be seen for design. Principles and methods that give precedence to the siting and specific area. This is an act of knowledge of the context *that comes out of its architectural modification* [my italics]. The origin of architecture is not the primitive hut, the cave or the mythical "Adam's House in Paradise." Before transforming a support into a column, roof into a tympanum, before placing stone on stone, man placed a stone on the ground to recognize a site in the midst of an unknown universe, in order to take account of it and modify it. As with every act of assessment, this one required radical moves and apparent simplicity. From this point of view, there are only two important attitudes to the context. The tools of the first are mimesis, organic imitation and the display of

complexity. The tools of the second are the assessment of physical relations, formal definition and interiorization of complexity.[11]

With the tectonic in mind it is possible to posit a revised account of the history of modern architecture, for when this trajectory is reinterpreted through the lens of the tectonic, certain patterns emerge and others recede. In this way a tectonic impulse may be traced across divers works of the past century irrespective of their different origins. In this process well-known affinities are further reinforced, while others recede and hitherto unremarked connections emerge asserting the importance of criteria that lie to one side of superficial stylistic differences. Thus, for all their stylistic idiosyncrasies, a very similar level of tectonic articulation patently links Hendrik Petrus Berlage's Stock Exchange of 1895 to Frank Lloyd Wright's Larkin Building (fig. 1.2) of 1904 and Herman Hertzberger's Central Beheer office complex of 1974 (fig. 1.3). In each instance there is a similar concatenation of span and support that amounts to a tectonic syntax in which gravitational force passes from purlin to truss, to pad stone, to corbel, to arch, to pier and abutment. The technical transfer of this load passes through a series of appropriately articulated transitions and joints. In each of these works the constructional articulation engenders the spatial subdivision and vice versa, and this same principle may be found in other works of this century possessing quite different stylistic aspirations. Thus we find a comparable concern for the revealed joint in the architecture of both Auguste Perret and Louis Kahn. In each instance the joint guarantees the probity and presence of the overall form while alluding to distinct different ideological and referential antecedents. While Perret looks back to the structurally rationalized classicism of the Graeco-Gothic ideal, dating back in France to the beginning of the eighteenth century, Kahn seems to evoke a timeless archaism, at once technologically advanced but spiritually antique.

The case can be made that the prime inspiration behind all this work stemmed as much from Eugène Viollet-le-Duc as from Semper, although clearly Wright's conception of built form as a petrified fabric writ large, most evident in his textile block houses of the 1920s, derives directly from the cultural priority that Semper gave to textile production and to the knot as the primordial tectonic unit. Aside from the common typological culture of the École des Beaux Art uniting all three, it is arguable that Kahn was as much influenced by Wright as by the Structural Rationalist line stemming from Viollet-le-Duc. This particular genealogy enables us to recognize the links tying Kahn's Richards Laboratories of 1959 back to Wright's Larkin Building. In each instance there is a similar "tartan," textile-like preoccupation with dividing the enclosed volume and its various appointments into "servant" and "served" spaces. In addition, there is a very similar concern for the *expressive rendering of mechanical services* as though they were of the same hierarchic importance as the structural frame. Thus the monumental brick ventilation shafts of the Richards Laboratories (fig. 1.4) are anticipated, as it were, in the hollow, ducted brick bastions that establish the four-square monu-

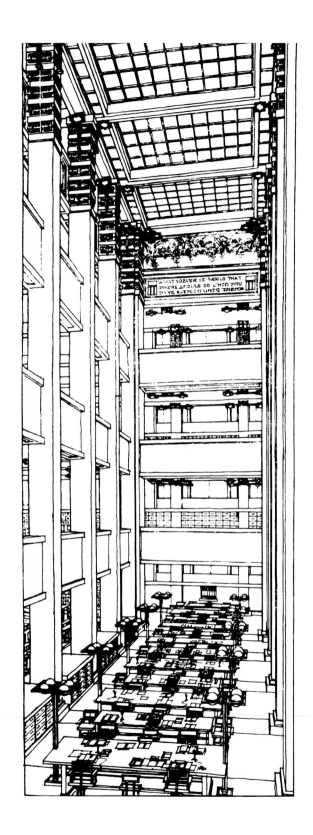

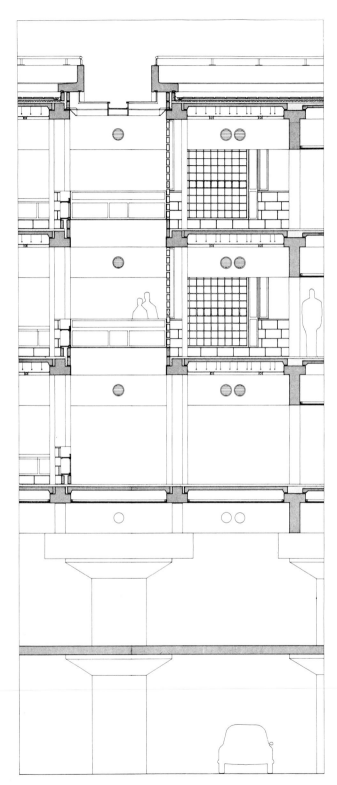

Fig. 1.2. (*Left*) Frank Lloyd Wright—Larkin Building, Buffalo, 1904. Interior view of top-lit central hall.

Fig. 1.3. Herman Hertzberger—Central Beheer, Apeldoorn, Holland, 1972. Cross-section through typical office space with garage space beneath.

mental corners of the Larkin Building (fig. 1.5). However dematerialized, there is a comparable discrimination between the servant and served spaces in Norman Foster's Sainsbury Centre of 1978, combined with a similar penchant for the expressive potential of mechanical services (fig. 1.6). And here again we encounter further proof that the tectonic in the twentieth century cannot concern itself only with structural form.

Wright's highly tectonic approach and the influence of this on the later phases of the modern movement has been underestimated, for Wright is surely the primary influence behind such diverse European figures as Carlo Scarpa, Franco Albini, Leonardo Ricci, Gino Valle, and Umberto Riva, to cite only the Italian Wrightian line. A similar Wrightian connection runs through Scandinavia and Spain, serving to connect such diverse figures as Jorn Utzon, Xavier Saenz de Oiza, and most recently Rafael Moneo, who as it happens was a pupil of both Utzon and Saenz de Oiza.

Something has to be said of the crucial role played by the joint in the work of Scarpa and to note the syntactically tectonic nature of his architecture. This dimension has been brilliantly characterized by Marco Frascari in his essay on the mutual reciprocity of "constructing" and "construing."

Fig. 1.4. Louis Kahn — Richards Laboratories, Philadelphia, 1957–61. Early sketch for ventilation towers; note the towers increase in section as they rise as opposed to the columns that conversely grow fatter as they descend.

15

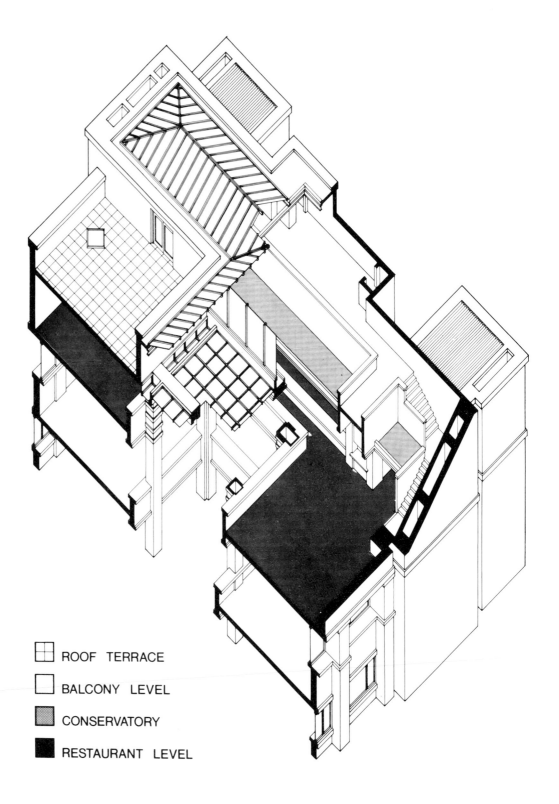

Fig. 1.5. Frank Lloyd Wright—Larkin Building, Buffalo, 1904. Axonometric of the fifth floor, restaurant and kitchen levels, as drawn by James Cahill. Note the service ducts built into the corner bastion.

Fig. 1.6. (*Facing page*) Norman Foster—Sainsbury Centre for the Visual Arts, Norwich, England, 1978. Half-cross-section through gallery with glass fixing details.

ROOF TERRACE

BALCONY LEVEL

CONSERVATORY

RESTAURANT LEVEL

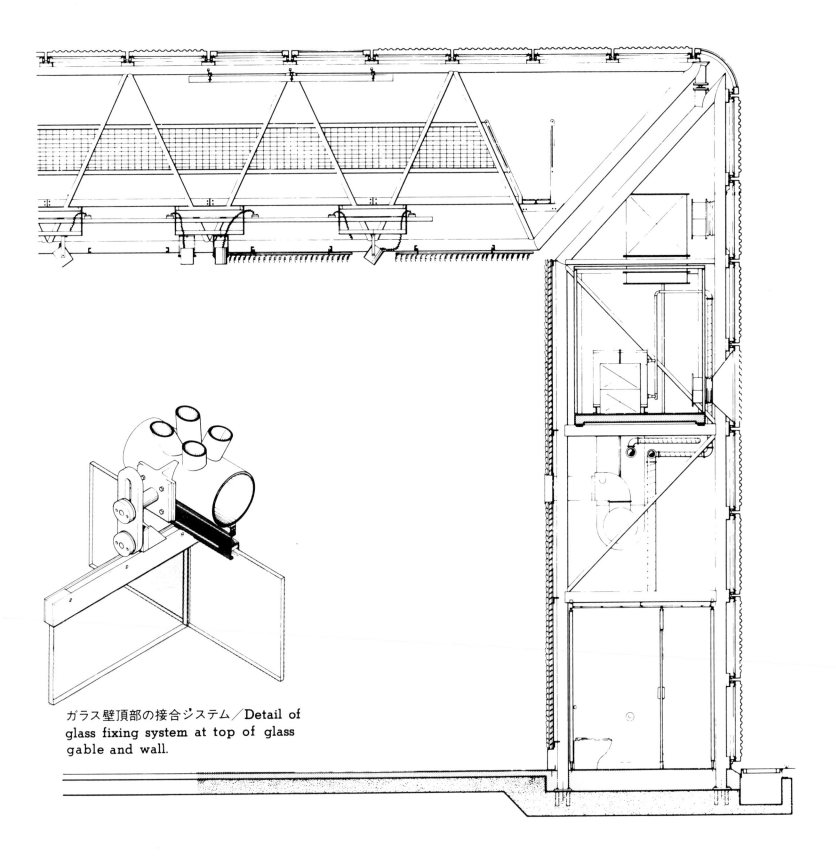

ガラス壁頂部の接合システム／Detail of
glass fixing system at top of glass
gable and wall.

Technology is a strange word. It has always been difficult to define its semantic realm. Through changes in meaning, at different times and in different places, of the word "technology" into its original components of *techne* and *logos,* it is possible to set up a mirror-like relationship between the *techne* of *logos* and the *logos* of *techne.* At the time of the Enlightenment the rhetorical *techne* of *logos* was replaced by the scientific *logos* of *techne.* However, in Scarpa's architecture this replacement did not take place. Technology is present with both the forms in a chiasmatic quality. Translating this chiasmatic presence into a language proper to architecture is like saying that there is no construction without a construing, and no construing without a construction.[12]

Elsewhere Frascari writes of the irreducible importance of the joint not only for the work of Scarpa but for all tectonic endeavors. Thus we read in a further essay entitled "The Tell-Tale Detail":

> Architecture is an art because it is interested not only in the original need for shelter but also in putting together spaces and materials, in a meaningful manner. This occurs through formal and actual joints. The joint, that is the fertile detail, is the place where both the construction and the construing of architecture takes place. Furthermore, it is useful to complete our understanding of this essential role of the joint as the place of the process of signification to recall that the meaning of the original Indo-European root of the word *art* is joint.[13]

If the work of Scarpa assumes paramount importance for its stress on the joint (fig. 1.7), the seminal value of Utzon's contribution to the evolution of modern tectonic form resides in his unconscious interpretation of Semper's four elements. This is particularly evident in all his "podium/pagoda" paradigm as this comes to be articulated throughout his career into the earthwork, the great floating roof, and a textile-like infill between the two (*Die Wand*), irrespective of whether the crowning roof element comprises a shell vault or a folded slab (cf. the Sydney Opera House of 1973, and the Bagsvaerd Church of 1977). It says something for Moneo's apprenticeship under Utzon that a similar articulation of earthwork and roof is evident in Moneo's Roman Archaeological Museum completed in Merida, Spain, in 1986 (fig. 1.8).

As we have already indicated, the tectonic lies suspended between a series of opposites, above all between the ontological and the representational. However, other dialogical conditions are involved in the articulation of tectonic form, particularly the contrast between the culture of the heavy—stereotomics—and the culture of the light—tectonics. The first implies load-bearing masonry that tends towards the earth and opacity. The second implies the dematerialized frame and tends towards the sky and translucence. At one end of this scale we have Semper's earthwork reduced in primordial times, as Gregotti reminds us, to the marking of

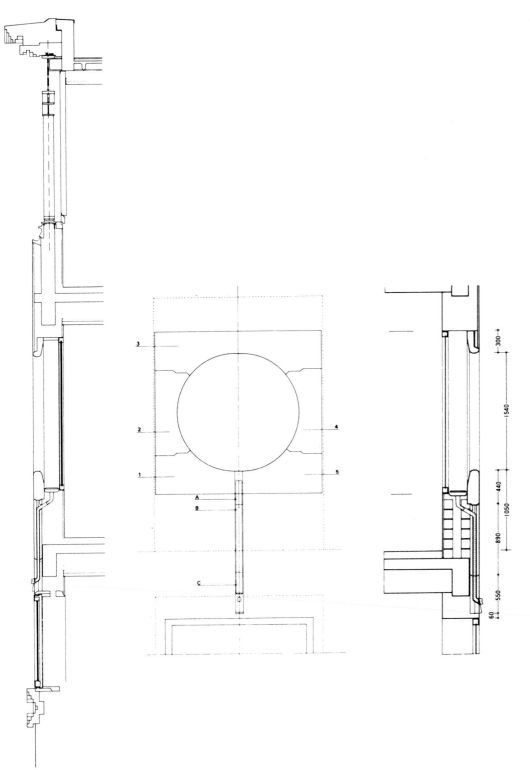

Fig. 1.7. Carlo Scarpa
—Banco Popolare di
Verona, Verona, Italy,
1973–84. Cross-section
through the main
facade.

19

ground. At the other end we have the ethereal, dematerialized aspirations of Joseph Paxton's Crystal Palace, that which Le Corbusier once described as the victory of light over gravity.

Since few works are absolutely one thing or the other, it can be claimed that the poetics of construction arise, in part, out of the inflection and positioning of the two primary dialogical objects of all tectonic form. Thus the earthwork extends itself upwards as walling to become an arch or a vault, or alternatively withdraws first to become the cross-wall support for a simple lightweight span and then to become a podium, elevated from the earth, on which an entire framework takes its anchorage. The converse applies in all timber construction where the framework extends itself to incorporate a suspended timber platform, as in the traditional Japanese house. The earthwork is now reduced to nothing but pad foundations. Other polarities serve to articulate this dialogical movement further, such as smooth versus rough, at the level of material (cf. Adrian Stokes) or dark versus light, at the level of illumination.

Finally, something has to be said about the signification of the "break" or the "dis-joint" as opposed to that of the joint. I am alluding to that point at which things break against each other rather than connect: that significant fulcrum at which one system, surface, or material abruptly ends to give way to another. Meaning may thus be encoded through the interplay between joint and break, and in this regard rupture may have just as much meaning as connection. Such considerations sensitize the architecture to the semantic risks that attend all forms of articulation, ranging from over-articulation of joints to under-articulation of form.

Postscript: Tectonic Form and Critical Culture
As Sigfried Giedion was to remark in the introduction to his two-volume study *The Eternal Present* (1962), among the deeper impulses of modern culture in the first half of the twentieth century was a desire to return to the timelessness of a prehistoric past: to recover in a literal sense some dimension of an eternal present, lying outside the nightmare of history and beyond the processal compulsions of instrumental progress. This drive insinuates itself again today as a potential ground from which to resist the commodification of culture. Within architecture the tectonic suggests itself as a mythical category with which to acquire entry to an antiprocessal world wherein the "presencing" of things may again facilitate the appearance of Being and experience of men. Beyond the *aporias* of the history of progress and outside the reactionary closures of historicism and the neo-avant-garde, lies the potential for a marginal counterhistory. This is the primeval history of the *logos* to which Giambattista Vico addressed himself, in his *Nuova Scienza,* in an attempt to adduce the poetic logic of institutional form. It is a mark of the radical nature of Vico's thought that he insisted that knowledge is not just the province of objective fact but also the consequence of a subjective,

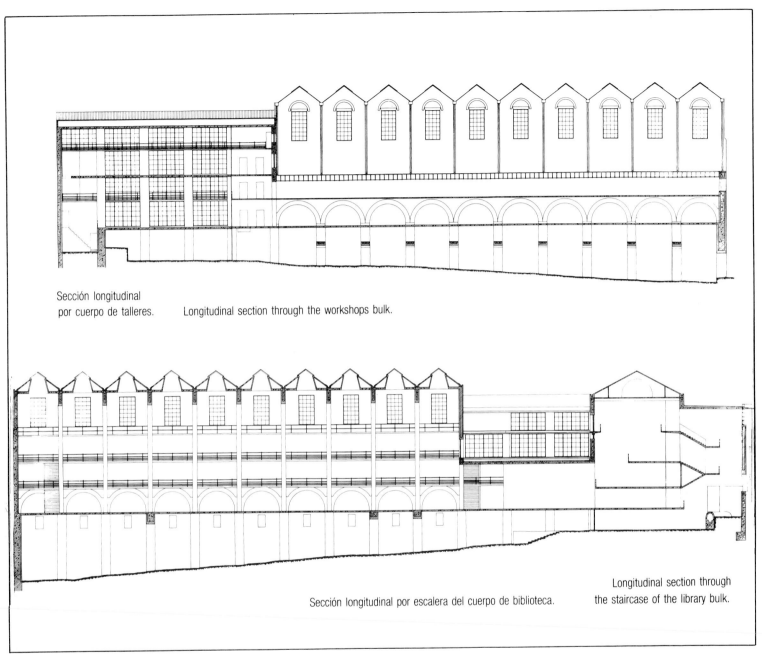

Sección longitudinal
por cuerpo de talleres.   Longitudinal section through the workshops bulk.

Sección longitudinal por escalera del cuerpo de biblioteca.   Longitudinal section through
the staircase of the library bulk.

Fig. 1.8. Rafael Moneo—Roman Archaeological Museum, Merida, Spain, 1980–85. Cross-section showing earthwork and folded monitor roof.

collective elaboration of archetypal myth. The critical myth of the tectonic joint points to just this timeless, time-bound moment, excised from the continuity of time.

Notes

1. Hans Sedlmayr, *Art in Crisis: The Lost Centre* (New York and London: Hollis and Carter Spottiswoode, Ballantyne & Co. Ltd., (1957), 164.

2. Clement Greenberg, "Modern Painting," 1965. Republished in *The New Art,* ed. Gregory Battcock (New York: Dalton, 1966), 101–102.

3. Giorgio Grassi, "Avant-Garde and Continuity," *Oppositions* 21 (Summer, 1980): 26–27.

4. Ignasi Sola Morales, "Critical Discipline," *Oppositions* 23 (Winter, 1981): 148–50.

5. K. O. Müller, *Ancient Art and Its Remains; or, a Manual of the Archaeology of Art,* (London: 1850).

6. Karl Botticher, *Die Tektonik der Hellenen,* 2 vols. (Potsdam: 1844–52); *Die Vier Elemente der Bankunst; Ein Beitrag zur vergleichenden Bankunde* (Brannschweig: Viewig, 1851).

7. *Der Stil in den technischen und tektonischen Kunsten oder praletische Aesthetik,* 2 vols. (Munich: Bruckmann, 1860–63).

8. Gottfried Semper, *Theorie der Formell-Schören,* ca 1856–59. Ms. 179. Fols. 1–46 in Semper Archive, GTE/ETH, Zurich. For English translation of introduction to this thesis, see pp. 219–44.

9. Pierre Bourdieu, "The Berber Home or the World Reversed," *Social Science Information,* vol. 9, no. 2 (1969): 151–70.

10. Karl Gruber, *Die Gestalt der deutschen Stadt* (Munich: Callwey, 1952).

11. Vittorio Gregotti, "Lecture at the New York Architectural League," *Section A* 1:1 (Feb./Mar., 1983), Montreal, Canada.

12. Marco Frascari, "A New Angel-Angle in Architectural Research: The Ideas of Demonstration," first draft of article subsequently published in *Journal of Architectural Education* (Nov., 1990).

13. Marco Frascari, "The Tell-Tale Detail," *VIA* 7 (1984): 23–37.

Time, Death, and Building

Karsten Harries

Architecture has been understood as the art of establishing place by bounding space.[1] Such understanding suggests the traditional division of the arts, going back to Lessing's *Laocoon,* into arts of space and arts of time. Lessing drew this distinction in order to reject the Horatian dictum that a poem ought to be like a picture: *ut pictura poesis.* In this rejected view both poet and painter paint, one with colors, the other with words; both poetry and painting are arts of representation, distinguished only by their medium. Challenging this understanding, Lessing insisted on their profound difference: "I argue thus. If it be true that painting employs wholly different signs or means of imitation from poetry—the one using forms and colors in space, the other articulate sounds in time—and if signs must unquestionably stand in convenient relation with the thing signified, then signs arranged side by side can represent only objects existing side by side, or whose parts succeed each other, in time."[2]

Lessing broadens his questionable argument to distinguish between arts of space and arts of time, between formative and expressive arts, and therefore also between arts of presence and arts of absence. Painting, sculpture, and architecture are included among the former, poetry and music among the latter. Because they are involved with space, the formative arts are limited to stable forms; they should not attempt to express what is essentially transitory. Their beauty is thought in opposition to time: "All phenomena, whose nature it is suddenly to break out and as suddenly to disappear, which can remain as they are but for a moment; all such phenomena, whether agreeable or otherwise, acquire through the perpetuity conferred upon them by art such an unnatural appearance, that the impression they produce becomes weaker with every fresh observation till the whole subject at last wearies or disgusts us."[3] So understood, the visual arts confer perpetuity: they preserve at least a semblance of eternity.

Obvious as such a distinction may seem, it is easy to think of examples that call it into question. The very fact that we speak of expressionist art, and even of expressionist architecture, makes one wonder. Is expressionism in some sense deficient because it engages time? Take abstract expressionism: here the painting presents traces of an action; it gestures beyond itself to its absent origin. Something of the temporal quality of that action is preserved by what appears on the canvas. Apart from the temporal significance of style, the different ways in which we experience a painting, a sculpture, or a work of architecture place us in different relationships to time. We stand before a picture; most sculptures invite us to change our position, perhaps even to walk around them; architecture not only invites us to change our position, but to enter and move around within it.

Generalizing, we can say that body and body awareness become more important as we turn from painting to sculpture to architecture. Take the example of a painting that obeys all the rules of one-point perspective. Such a work presupposes a specific point of view. Ideally, it should be seen only with one eye, through a peep-hole, as Brunelleschi showed when he demonstrated his new system of perspective.[4] As a matter of fact, when we look at such a painting we never quite meet these conditions. We use two eyes, our eyes move, and we move as we observe the painting. Yet all this matters little to our experience of the painting. Experience remains focused on the self-sufficient esthetic object, not on our relationship to it. Absorbed in the artwork, we forget time.

Michael Fried calls attention to one class of works that involve time in a very different way: "The connection between spatial recession and some such experience of temporality—almost as if the first were a kind of natural metaphor for the second—is present in much Surrealist painting (e.g., De Chirico, Dali, Tanguy, Magritte). Moreover, temporality—manifested, for example, as expectation, dread, anxiety, presentiment, memory, nostalgia, stasis—is often the explicit subject of their painting."[5] Fried calls art that would thus communicate some experience of temporality "theatrical" and opposed it to another that strives to transcend time in order to pursue *presentness.* Following the ideal of the timeless self-sufficiency of the art object that has come to dominate both the theory and the practice of art since the eighteenth century, Fried considers only the art of presentness as the legitimate art of modernity. Temporal art is condemned in a way strictly analogous to the way in which so many Neoclassicists of the eighteenth century condemned Rococo and Baroque art for its theatricality. Peter Eisenmann is right to associate the classical with presentness and timelessness: beauty against time. And so understood, classicism includes modernism.[6]

Our experience of sculpture involves the body in a more obvious way than does painting; most sculpture invites us to explore it by moving past it. Robert Morris celebrates the observer's relationship to sculpture; his best new work lets observers recognize that they themselves are establishing relationships as they "apprehend the object from various positions and under varying conditions of light and spatial context."[7] Sculpture, we may say, is more intimately tied to time than painting. Using Fried's terminology, we may say that while there is much theatri-

cal sculpture—Bernini provides often-cited examples—other sculpture pursues
the ideal of presentness. By the strength of its configuration of forms such sculpture renders our point of view unimportant. To Fried, the works of David Smith
and Anthony Caro exemplify genuinely modernist sculpture.[8]

In a more obvious way, architecture is experienced by the moving body: we approach a building, walk by or around it, perhaps enter it. Recall that Fried says
spatial recession in painting offers "a kind of natural metaphor" for the "experience of temporality." In actual space, our understanding of recession and, more
generally, of distance is inseparable from an anticipation of how long it would
take us to walk down that aisle or to cross that square. In our experience of architecture, point of view and the possibility of changing it are crucially important.

If we characterize painting, sculpture, and architecture in terms of their different
relationships to time, it is important not to make such characterizations too
rigid. Just as there is no constant relationship of architecture to time, so there is
no constant relationship of architecture to painting and sculpture. There is architecture that, like some Renaissance paintings, invites or even prescribes a specific
point of view: Baroque and Rococo architecture provide countless examples.

Other architecture may invite us to explore a sequence of points of view. Consider how Eero Saarinen shaped the passage between Morse and Stiles colleges
at Yale into a shifting frame for the Gothic tower of Payne Whitney Gymnasium.
This example of the picturesque invites the observer to stop and look, but not for
too long. Part of our pleasure lies in how, as we walk, changing points of view
yield new pictures. The late eighteenth century especially embraced the picturesque and thus time. In countless English parks we find follies—an artificial ruin,
a classicizing temple, or a grave monument—designed not so much to be entered
as to be experienced in a pictorial way by someone walking through the park;
significantly, the experienced "picture" is itself not a fully present esthetic object,
but haunted by the absence of a past plenitude now denied to us.

The same concern for the "picture" can also govern interiors, as in some Baroque
and Rococo church architecture. In the Augustinian priory church at Diessen,
frescoes spanning the nave play a crucial part in pictorializing interior space. The
privileged point of view near the entrance allows us to experience not just the
fresco but the whole interior as a pictorial composition having its center at the
high altar.[9] The strength of this "picture" arrests us and invites contemplation.
But this invitation is counteracted by the pull of other points of view that beckon
to be explored.

A contemporary example of the picturesque is Louis Kahn's British Art Center at
Yale University. The task of building a gallery to house framed pictures provided
Kahn with an occasion to explore and play with the idea of frame and framing:

framed pictures are in turn framed by the architecture; spectators are framed; Kahn's windows frame the Old Art Gallery across the street, now visible as never before.

Comparable to pictorial architecture is architecture that we experience as a self-sufficient piece of sculpture: think of the pyramids. Kevin Roche's Knights of Columbus Building in New Haven has a kind of sculptural quality that almost allows us to forget its interior. Roche conceived the building and its basic geometry in relation to the moving traffic of the Connecticut Turnpike as a stable beacon in a restless world, seeking both monumentality and presentness. Together with the adjoining Coliseum's strong horizontal, the Knights of Columbus Building recalls medieval cathedrals with strong, vertical towers and sheltering horizontal roofs. How difficult it remains to build monumental architecture that does not evoke either churches or temples! Despite the strength of their seemingly timeless forms, time enters such buildings after all as the present is haunted by the absent plenitude of an idealized past.

I have suggested that architecture, too, may be considered an art of time: whether it does so deliberately or not, architecture cannot but shape our experience of time. To give more focus to this point let me turn to Wölfflin's *Principles of Art History* as they apply to architecture.

1. First of all, Wölfflin distinguished between the *linear* and the *painterly,* or, more generally, between the *unpainterly* and the *painterly.* "The elementary phenomenon is this—that two totally different architectural effects are produced according to whether we are obliged to perceive the architectural form as something definite, solid, enduring, or as something over which, for all its stability, there plays an apparent, constant movement, that is change."[10]

Whenever architecture is experienced as a picture, there is a certain "derealization," as what is three-dimensional is challenged in its solid three-dimensionality. Rust stains on concrete or the texture of aged bricks evokes the passage of time. In this connection we should also keep in mind the importance of changing light. While direct sunlight gives definition and solidity to what it strikes, indirect light dematerializes and renders what it illuminates weightless and evanescent.

Linear and painterly, as analyzed by Wölfflin, stand in different relationships to time: in the case of the painterly he speaks of the play of an apparent constant movement, while linear architecture is said to be experienced as definite, solid, and enduring. Painterly architecture thus embraces time, while linear architecture reaches beyond time to the plenitude of a timeless present.

2. Essentially the same relationship holds for Wölfflin's other paired principles. Take the second pair: *plane* and *recession.* Wölfflin himself raises an obvious

objection to the application of this principle to architecture. Recalling Fried's understanding of recession as a natural metaphor of temporality, does not architecture always depend on recession? "Planimetric architecture" sounds dangerously like nonsense.[11] And yet the point of his distinction is clear enough:

> What else is it but a deviation from frontality when the posts of the porch of a villa no longer look forwards but turn towards each other? With what other words can we describe the process which the altar passes through in which a purely frontal construction becomes more and more interspersed with recessional elements until, in the end, in rich baroque churches, there stand enclosures which draw the essence of their interest from the recession of the forms? And if we analyze the plan of the baroque staircase and terrace, such as the Spanish Steps in Rome, not to speak of any other detail, the spatial recession is brought out merely by the multiple orientation of the steps in such a way that the classically strict layout with straight flights looks flat beside it.[12]

3. Wölfflin's next pair opposed *closed* or *tectonic* to *open* or *a-tectonic* form:

> The tectonic style is the style of strict arrangement and clear adherence to rule: the a-tectonic, on the other hand, is the style of more or less concealed adherence to rule and of free arrangement. In the former case, the vital nerve in every effect is the inevitability of the organization, absolute immutability. In the latter, art plays with the semblance of the lawless. It plays, for in an aesthetic sense, of course, form is bound by necessity in all art, but the baroque tends to conceal the rule, loosens the frames and joints, introduces dissonance, and, in decoration verges on the impression of the casual.[13]

We may question whether play in art is always bound by necessity. Clearly the open or a-tectonic form means freedom, openness, mutability. The turn from modern to Postmodern architecture may be characterized as a turn from closed to open form. Ambiguity, complexity, and contradiction in architecture belong with open form. It would thus be easy to draw parallels between Baroque or Rococo and Postmodern architecture, as Venturi has done.[14]

4. Wölfflin's fourth pair, *multiplicity* and *unity,* does not quite name what he has in mind. He contrasts an architecture of multiplicity that constructs an architectural whole out of parts that retain their separate identities and an independent value not swallowed up in the larger whole, as opposed to another architecture of unity that strives to create wholes that are more integrated, organic, and difficult to grasp. "No longer do beautiful elements combine in a unity in which they continue to breathe independently, but the parts have submitted to a dominating total motive, and only the cooperation with the whole gives them sense and beauty."[15] The cruciform church plan as used by Brunelleschi offers a good example of the former; its Rococo transformation by Balthasar Neumann illustrates the latter, yielding a mysterious space haunted by absence.

5. Finally, Wölfflin opposes *clearness* to *unclearness* or *absolute* to *relative clearness*. Once again he develops his pair by contrasting classical with Baroque architecture.

> In the one case, form which is completely apparent: in the other, a creation which is, it is true, clear enough not to trouble the eye, but still not so clear that the spectator could ever reach the end. In this type late Gothic proceeded beyond high Gothic, the baroque beyond the classic Renaissance. It is not true that man can only take delight in the absolutely clear: he at once desires to get away from the clear to what can never be exhausted by visual perception. However manifold the post-renaissance transformations of style may be, they all have this remarkable quality, that the picture in some way eludes perfect comprehensibility.[16]

The transformations Wölfflin has in mind all tend towards an architecture that refuses the ideal of readily comprehended form, insisting on absence rather than presence. Of course there have always been reactions to such developments: one is Neoclassicism, which in turn provoked a romantic counter-reaction, and there is a good deal of romanticism in nineteenth-century eclecticism. Modernism reasserted the classical ideal; Postmodernism the Baroque reaction.

You will have noted how difficult it is to speak of any of these pairs without drawing on all the others. It is thus possible to combine them and to contrast an *a-tectonic, organic* approach to architecture with a *tectonic, inorganic* approach. Using the terms broadly, we can call the former "Baroque," the latter "classical." The former invites metaphors that suggest absence, change, life, time; the latter invokes metaphors that suggest presence, stasis, death, eternity. In this way Wölfflin's principles show that architectural style communicates a particular relationship to time and thereby a particular ethos, as I have shown in my book on the Bavarian Rococo church. We can, at any rate, distinguish an architecture that sets itself up against time, defying it, from one that embraces it.

I have tried to question the distinction between arts of space and arts of time, to show that time is as intimately involved in our experience of architecture as space. The two indeed cannot be separated. This is to say also that any understanding of architecture as an establishment of place by bounding space is necessarily one-sided. If dwelling requires the establishment of place, place must also be understood temporally.[17] Heidegger's famous description of a Black Forest farmhouse insists thus not only on the spatial, but also on the temporal dimensions of dwelling and building.

> The nature of building is letting dwell. Building accomplishes its essential nature in the raising of locations by the joining of their spaces. *Only if we are capable of dwelling, only then can we build.* Let us think for a while of a farmhouse in the Black Forest, which was built some two hundred years ago by the dwelling of peasants. Here the self-sufficiency of the power to let earth and heaven, divinities and mortals enter *in simple oneness* into things,

ordered the house. It placed the farm on the wind-sheltered mountain-slope looking south, among the meadows close to the spring. It gave it the wide overhanging shingle roof whose proper slope bears up under the burden of snow, and which, reaching deep down, shields the chambers against the storms of the long winter nights. It did not forget the altar corner behind the community table; it made room in its chamber for the hallowed places of childbed and the "tree of the dead"—for that is what they call a coffin there: the *Totenbaum*—and in this way it designed for the different generations under one roof the character of their journey through time. A craft which, itself sprung from the dwelling, still uses its tools and frames as things, built the farmhouse.[18]

Here we have a building that embraces time: the rhythm of the seasons, of the passing generations, of birth, and of death. I want to underscore the emphasis placed on the way the house gives room to death. If building is to let us dwell, in Heidegger's sense, it must grant death its place. This is also to say: only those will be capable of genuine building who have affirmed themselves as the mortals they are. Dwelling in this view presupposes authentic being unto death, as Heidegger had analyzed it in *Being and Time*. But Heidegger also knows the difficulty human beings, and especially we moderns, have in accepting death. The whole classical tradition with its celebration of plenitude and presentness testifies to this difficulty. That Fried should have made the pursuit of presentness constitutive of what he takes to be the only authentic art of our time could not have surprised Heidegger, although he would have added that, so understood, "authentic art" is a manifestation of inauthenticity.

There are places where Heidegger suggests that we moderns have become altogether incapable of the kind of dwelling that built the Black Forest farmhouse, and to relearn the art of dwelling we have to take our leave from modernism, and also from the classical tradition. We have become incapable of genuine dwelling because we have become incapable of really dying. For this to make sense, we have to distinguish what Heidegger calls dying from what we usually mean by the term. Death here cannot simply mean the end of life. "To die," according to Heidegger, "means to carry out death in its essence. To be able to die means to be capable of this carrying out."[19] In *Being and Time* Heidegger ties authentic existence to this ability. But the Second World War, especially, taught Heidegger that circumstances can make authentic dying impossible. "Do they die?" Heidegger asks of those who perish in extermination camps. "Hardly noticed," they are "cut down, liquidated."[20] But the inhumanity that so horribly manifested itself in the Nazis' factories of death cannot simply be relegated to the past as a uniquely monstrous aberration. It is rooted, if Heidegger is right, in the technological essence of modernity, which threatens to reduce all that is, including human beings, to material to be used and used up.

turning lathes. The twentieth century with its machine technology has allowed us to envision beauties Plato could not have dreamed of.

But the main point remains the same: the Platonic idealization of beauty of geometric forms leads easily to a machine esthetic. The machine-made object, the machine-made look is given the nod precisely because it bears the imprint of the human spirit. It allows us to feel at home, as the organic does not.

The pursuit of the plenitude of being expresses itself in a choice of particular forms and also, as Plato points out, in a choice of particular colors. Primary colors have a timeless quality, compared with broken greens and browns, which hint at the changing earth. Also building materials, such as wood or brick, that age gracefully stand in a very different relationship to time than vinyl siding or formica. Created by human beings, the machine-made environment looks human as the natural environment does not. Someone might retort: isn't such a machine-made environment just the opposite, inhuman rather than human precisely because it excludes or reduces traces of the body? Both claims are easily defended; they presuppose different conceptions of human existence. If the machine-made environment is experienced as more human than the natural environment, this presupposes that human being has been identified with the "spirit." If, on the other hand, such an environment is dismissed as inhuman, this presupposes that the human being is understood more concretely as essentially an embodied self, which cannot hope to find refuge from the terror of time in abstract realms of the spirit without losing itself.

In the twentieth century this Platonism has come close to evolving into the esthetic of the modern movement, witness this statement from the manifesto "Purism," by Le Corbusier and Ozenfant: "Nothing is worthwhile which is not general, nothing is worthwhile which is not transmittable. We have attempted to establish an esthetic that is rational, and therefore human."[24] What is worthwhile in art is identified here with what is rational; the rational is essentially general and in principle can be understood by everyone.

> It is true that plastic art has to address itself more directly to the senses than pure mathematics which only acts by symbols, these symbols sufficing to trigger in the mind consequences of a superior order; in plastic art, the sense should be strongly moved in order to predispose the mind to the release into play of subjective reactions without which there is no work of art. But there is no art worth having without this excitement of an intellectual order, of a mathematical order; architecture is the art which up until now has most strongly induced the states of this category. The reason is that everything in architecture is expressed by order and economy.[25]

The spirit provides a timelessly valid vocabulary on which artists can draw to create art of universal significance.

Theo van Doesburg explains the preference for machine-produced materials and forms: "Every machine is a spiritualization of an organism. . . . The machine is, *par excellence,* a phenomenon of spiritual discipline. . . . The new artistic sensibility of the twentieth century has not only felt the beauty of the machine, but has also taken cognizance of its unlimited expressive possibilities for the arts."[26] Craft and the hand have no place in the art that is being envisioned here. Clearly such an esthetic implies a downgrading of the individual. But a convinced modernist will hail the machine and the new spirituality as positive forces that break down national and class boundaries and destroy the cult of the individual.

Does such an esthetic do justice to human reality? Does it offer more than alienating metaphors of an impossible perfection?

The need to rethink the modernist love affair with technology, especially as it pertains to architecture, is illuminated by an unfinished story by Franz Kafka, called "Der Bau" (The Building). Since the story's protagonist is an animal—we are not told what kind—"The Den" or "The Burrow" might be a better translation.[27] What strikes the reader of the story first of all is a certain mood, a sense of helplessness and hopelessness, bound up with this animal's impossible desire for total security. Feared, suspected, but unseen enemies lead it to think of ever more elaborate defenses. Here building becomes a weapon against the terror of time. But whatever defenses the animal constructs, construction is outstripped by thoughts of other, still unmastered threats. Dedicated to the pursuit of security, its life is shadowed by what will not be mastered. Unable to possess and master its environment, the animal attempts to withdraw into the artificial environment it has constructed. But the threatening outside, and the still unmastered future, cannot be eliminated by fleeing inside. Because it cannot be grasped and controlled, what is hidden weighs on the animal: the outside where the animal's control ceases. Every noise comes to be experienced as a threat, absolute quiet is sought as an assurance of security. But certain noises will not be eliminated, especially a barely audible, curious hissing that seems to indicate the hidden presence of some death-dealing enemy.

Who is this animal? Obviously not an ordinary animal; this animal reasons. *Animal rationale* is one traditional definition of the human being. The animal of Kafka's story, however, is not just a figure of the human animal, but of the human animal unable to accept being an animal, who gets hungry, experiences sexual desire, and must die. Essentially embodied, subject to time, we are unable to provide the measure of security that we demand. That demand would be fulfilled only if we could truly assert ourselves as "the masters and possessors" of nature.[28]

As Descartes had already recognized when he promised such mastery, it calls for all-embracing technological control. Presupposed by this call is a will to power that cannot forgive itself its final lack of power and cannot forgive itself its own embodied, temporal being, and precisely because of this experiences so keenly the terror of time, has such difficulty accepting the reality of death, is unable to die in Heidegger's sense. The human will to power, when it cannot accept its final lack of power, has to give birth to what Nietzsche called "the spirit of revenge" against time, for that ill will "against time and its 'it was,'" which is a presupposition of modernist esthetics.[29] But how can we cure ourselves of the spirit of revenge? The question proves inseparable from that other question: how are we to learn how to dwell?

Heidegger claims that to allow for genuine dwelling, building has to make room for death. The Black Forest farmhouse does this by giving space to the "hallowed places of childbed and the tree of the dead." Another house might have a special door reserved for such occasions. Pictures may serve to keep the dead present among the living. Sacred architecture has always had as one of its main tasks the illumination of life by facing the living with death. In church after church we find that bells, clocks, altars, and grave monuments sound their *memento mori*.[30] Or think of the social function of cemeteries, or of commemorative monuments, or of historical preservation.

Perhaps no building type has addressed the terror of time more self-consciously than the built ruin, which became a popular building type only in the eighteenth century. Here architecture seems to glory in its own inevitable destruction, as if the death of architecture were something to be desired. Interestingly enough, painters of that time began to imagine not-yet-ruined buildings in ruined condition: Hubert Robert, the Great Gallery of the Louvre; Caspar David Friedrich, the cathedral in Meissen and St. Jacobi in Greifswald.[31] Hitler is said to have had the architecture of his Thousand Year Empire drawn for himself as a ruin. Did he suspect how quickly reality would catch up with his dreams?

How are we to understand this fascination with ruins, this ambiguous response to our inability to take charge of nature, to assert ourselves as the masters of creation? The artificial ruin is a human construction that glories in the impermanence and instability of such construction. But why are we not crushed by the experience of the inevitable victory of time over building, of the cruel rule of nature's cycle of growth and decay, so indifferent to what we desire and hope for? One answer is given by the theory of the sublime. As Kant teaches, the delight we take in sublime sights testifies to human self-transcendence: our freedom cannot discover its true home in the finite. Our true self is not touched by destructive time. In the experience of the sublime a prideful self-assertion triumphs over destructive time.

But the artificial ruin also invites other, less prideful thoughts. Was it not pride, that same pride which cast Adam and Eve out of paradise, that lost us our place in nature and burdened us with mortality? The cult of ruins is linked to a tendency to see nature in the image of the lost paradise and architecture as an estrangement from that paradise. As architecture that deconstructs itself, the artificial ruin recalls us to what we have lost. Notwithstanding Rykwert's claim to the contrary, paradise had no need for architecture.[32] The Bible invites us to understand building as a response to the Fall, which faced human beings with an alien environment. Must not the attempt to replace that environment with our own construction be associated with sin? Architecture itself thus appears as a metaphor of pride, most powerfully in the tower of Babel. Indeed Cain, unlike his brother Abel, is already known as a builder of cities.

This distrust of the city of Cain still informs Frank Lloyd Wright's speculation in *The Living City:* "Go back far enough in time, mankind was divided into cave-dwelling agrarians and wandering tribes of hunter warriors. . . . The cave dweller became the cliff-dweller. He began to build cities. . . . His God was a malicious murderer. . . . He erected his God into a mysterious covenant. When he could, he made his God of gold."[33]

Note Wright's association of the necessarily sedentary life that agriculture brings with it with the emergence of the city, and the dehumanizing power of gold. This is the realm of Cain. Opposed to it is the realm of Abel: "But his swifter, more mobile brother, devised a more adaptable and elusive dwelling place—the folding tent. . . . He was the Adventurer. His God a spirit: devastating or beneficent as he was himself."[34]

The sedentary, rooted life is here understood as incompatible with spirituality. Humanity demands mobility. The modern city is placed by Wright closer to the tent-dwelling Abel than to the agrarian Cain. "So a human type is emerging capable of rapidly changing environment to fit desires, one amply able to offset the big city of today: Remnant of the great, ancient 'Wall.' In the capability to change we have a new type of citizen. We call him democratic."[35]

Wright makes an important point. Just as one can attack an excessive emphasis on roots and places as incompatible with human freedom, so one can question whether the emphasis on continuity and permanence does justice to human nature. Do we not require and demand change?

It is clear, however, that if this view is accepted, the city we have now, despite all our technological advances, will appear too burdened by the city of the past, by the city of Cain, to do justice to what Wright demands here.

But how are we to imagine the city of Abel?

In support of Wright's emphasis on the human capability to change is the widespread conviction that being is not solely a nature to be satisfied in fixed ways. Is it not only a small part of our needs that has its foundation in nature? Human needs have changed: our needs are no longer those of Heidegger's Black Forest farmer. What sense does it make, then, to appeal to a timeless ideal of dwelling?

Perhaps one can even argue that human beings need their needs to change. Suppose there were a fixed set of natural needs tied to hunger, sexual desire, and the need for shelter; and let us suppose further that all these needs were catered to and satisfied. Schopenhauer suggests that at this point boredom would take over. How then do we escape from boredom? Precisely by raising our needs beyond the natural level. Artificially induced needs take over as natural needs have been fulfilled. It is precisely this need to have needs which makes us so vulnerable to advertising and changing fashions. The new is interesting, where the interesting is defined as the not quite expected.

To what I called perennial Platonism we can thus oppose an esthetic of change best illustrated by popular art and fashion. Citing Reyner Banham, Jencks links this esthetic to a market- and consumer-oriented society: "It will be an aesthetic which will be 'used up' as fast as the product and quickly forgotten; an aesthetic which is based on popular images of power, sex, and other forms of social emulation, and an aesthetic which is above all popular, which will sell, which is always just one step ahead of the common dream—'on the frontier of the dream that money can just buy.'"[36]

In our time, needs are linked to what others consider important. The esthetic outlined by Jencks will thus retain contact with what is accepted and expected, but it will not settle for that because what everyone expects is boring. We shall therefore try to stay just a step ahead of the expected, not far enough to lose contact with it, but far enough to arouse interest, to titillate. The interesting has thus become a primary value in Postmodern architecture.[37] It bids us to stay just one step ahead of the common dream, where it is important that this dream be not altogether out of reach: the slightly too expensive car, stereo set, or house.

Such dreams do not have their foundation in idealizing memories that allow the past to figure the lost paradise, nor in recollections of some archetype. To a large extent these dreams are induced. The customer is led to buy what is not really needed. Whatever natural needs there may be have been absorbed and restructured by the market. It follows that the life of the commodity is short. The needs which it satisfies are themselves short-lived and soon give way to others. The objects that once satisfied them can then be discarded. The esthetic of change becomes the "throw-away esthetic."

Jencks gives the example of Peter and Alison Smithson, who took the Detroit-produced automobile for their model in designing their house for the future:
> In this case the pattern of a light, smooth, plastic shell divided by dark

joints [appears] much as a car is moulded and divided. The house could thus be cleaned as easily as the outside of a car, in as much as all the joints were curved and open to the 'electrostatic dust collector.' Furthermore, to continue the car analogy, a chrome strip streamlined the exterior and an annual model change was contemplated. There were also the car accessories or 'extras': the mobile service trolley dispensing favours like a benevolent robot, the pogo chair which could fold and stack, the mobile cooking articles which could be 'wander-plugged,' and the built-in storage cubicles which divided the areas *en suite* and closed out the household clutter with the flick of a concertina shutter.[38]

What is conjured up here may well strike us as a nightmare. No longer is the house a dwelling; it has become a machine that fills certain needs. The market has come to embrace life in its totality. Jencks might reply that our "mass production advertising" has indeed come to establish "our whole pattern of life— principles, aims, morals, aspirations and standard of living."[39] With this the human being becomes a plastic, endlessly malleable material. Responsibility and commitment lose their meaning, as does lasting community.

But why insist on the permanence of human associations? Why not think instead of the kind of instant communities created by a successful outdoor music festival or by a football game? Are all communities not more and more of this sort: not very long lasting, created by shared interests, and which we can join and leave with ease? The disintegration of marriage as an institution points in the same direction. With such an ethos, does it still make sense to insist on architecture in the traditional sense? Don't we need more flexible solutions? These will of necessity leave behind what architecture has traditionally been. Does modernity not demand communities that can be quickly put together, which hark back to the old paradigm of the tent? Much architecture today looks strangely mobile, as if ready to travel. Mobile home parks and the instant communities they create have paradigmatic significance.

More imaginative solutions were offered in the issues of the journal published by the *Archigram* team, a group of angry visionaries, working in London—utopian in the sense that the imagination here outstripped what could be realized. *Archigram* offered counter-images to the traditional city: a new city, held together by a relatively stable support structure, which would take care of plumbing, electricity, and the like, but which would allow for maximum flexibility with respect to location and the nature of dwelling.

Giedion and Doxiadis feared in such experiments a new inhumanity.[40] And yet, can the conviction to which these experiments answer not be defended with traditional arguments? We can go back to the idea of the tent-dwelling Abel, who shifted his home as his spirit moved him. Why should we remain stuck in one place? Do we not now possess a technology which finally allows us to satisfy our desire for novelty and change? Should an old-fashioned emphasis on continuity and timeless values be allowed to stand in the way?

On the other hand, Giedion and Doxiadis do seem to have a point: something seems to have gone drastically wrong when the ideal house is transformed into the kind of hemispherical standard living package envisioned by Reyner Banham: "But a properly set-up standard of living package, breathing out warm-air along the ground, . . . radiating soft light and Dionne Warwick in heart-warming stereo, with well-aged protein turning in an infra-red glow in the rotisserie, and the ice-maker discretely coughing cubes into glasses on the swing-out bar—this could do something for a woodland glade on creek-side rock that *Playboy* could never do for its penthouse. . . ."[41]

In these fantastic visions the artificial environment has become so responsive to the individual's needs that one can easily imagine an environment flexible enough to eliminate the need to move altogether. Playfully David Greene imagines a gigantic machine that will fulfill every need as it arises: "It's all the same. The joint between God-nodes and you, eat-nodes and you is the same. Theoretically, one node could service the lot. There's no need to move. Cool it baby! Be comfortable. Godburgers, sexburgers, hamburgers. The node just plugged into a giant needery. You sit there and need—we do the rest. Green stamps given."[42]

No doubt we have much to learn from *Archigram*'s attacks on the eternal and timeless. Both the body and the individual are shortchanged by perennial Platonism. But does this mean that we should exchange modernist universalism with a technological Postmodernism that not only recognizes, but welcomes the fact that conventions change, often within a short time span? Challenging such a conventionalism, I would insist that human nature has been stable enough throughout history to allow us to draw from an analysis of human being in the world a key to quite stable architectural symbols.[43] Does not the very fact that Plato and Mondrian share similar views on the beauty of certain forms and colors suggest that perennial Platonism cannot be dismissed as just another fashion? It does provide something like a language that transcends the particularities of time and place.

This is not to say that this language does justice to the entire human being. Elevated into an all-embracing esthetic, perennial Platonism does violence to the body, to the senses, and to the concrete person. An environment of such forms will leave us dissatisfied. Although this spiritual dimension is essential, its significance should not be exaggerated. Such exaggeration must lead to an overly abstract architecture that renders the concrete individual accidental. In the demand for an esthetic of change the legitimate claims of the embodied self make themselves heard.

But the utopian architecture celebrated in the issues of *Archigram* also involves repression. It hardly represents a joyful acceptance of the temporality of human dwelling. Quite the opposite: instead of an acceptance of time, *Archigram* reflects an attempt to escape the terror of time by losing oneself to present amusement. Don't plan too far ahead! Forget about death! Just recognize your needs and enjoy! Enjoy and forget yourself! Perennial Platonism with its esthetics of permanence and *Archigram*'s esthetic of change are linked by their dread of time; but when we cover up time we necessarily also cover up the person. Our sense of being a self is inseparable from an awareness that we must die.

Heidegger is right: architecture should speak to us of our mortality. The visions of *Archigram* dissolve the person into a collection of changing needs. Just as we can lose ourselves while absorbed in some television program, so David Greene's great needery would allow us to forget ourselves. The person disappears and with it community. Returning to the analogy with paradise: perhaps we can say that in paradise Adam and Eve were not yet persons in the full sense of the word. They became persons only when they wanted to know for themselves. But inseparable from such awakening is the recognition of human vulnerability and mortality, of the way our will to power is inevitably thwarted by our finitude. Thoughts of paradise or its analogue have always haunted us, but if we are to save our humanity they must remain thoughts or dreams. Any attempt to realize paradise on earth tends towards the destruction of the person. Genuine dwelling demands the renunciation of paradise.

But is there an architecture that instead of trying to take charge of time makes peace with it, open to both past and future? We are given a hint by Brueghel's painting of the Tower of Babel. The tower is of course a paradigm of an architecture of prideful self-assertion, but also of human impotence. Even as building goes on, the building becomes ruinous, reverting to landscape. But the tower is not the only building in the picture: there is the far less pretentious architecture of the surrounding city; and even the tower itself has become the setting for modest shelters that nestle against the walls, much as in medieval cities houses often lean against city walls or a church. Brueghel thus contrasts an architecture of pride with more modest buildings. We find the same contrast in Piranesi's views of Rome, which contrast the ruined grandeur of the ancients with houses that make up for their lack of grandeur with their humanity.

Building that permits genuine dwelling must give us a sense of security and yet recognize the impermanence of human life and construction. But am I not making here an impossible demand? How can a house do both: offer a sense of security and exhibit its own precariousness?

Bachelard gives us a pointer when he places genuine dwelling in opposition to a self-assertion that, in seeking to master the world, is unable to recognize the world as our first home, figured by all our other homes. Life, he insists, begins well, it begins "enclosed, protected, all warm in the bosom of the house."[44] It begins with confidence in the world, even though we have no reason for such confidence. "The experience of the hostility of the world—and consequently our dreams of defense and aggressiveness—come much later."[45] Only confidence in the world allows us to dwell. But it presupposes that we not take ourselves too seriously, that we learn to affirm ourselves as part of an unfolding generational order that extends from a past that is present only in traces, to an unknown future that hopefully will someday preserve our own traces. To help assure that this chain is not broken is one task of building. From this perspective it is easy to understand Adolf Loos's tendency to make the monument, especially the grave monument, the only remaining architectural task.

Notes

1. See, e.g., Paul Weiss, *Nine Basic Arts* (Carbondale: Southern Illinois University Press, 1961), 67–68. Also Karsten Harries, "Architecture and Ontology," in *Creativity and Common Sense: Essays in Honor of Paul Weiss,* ed. Thoms Krettek (Albany: State University of New York Press, 1987), 145–61.

2. Gotthold Ephraim Lessing, *Laocoon: An Essay Upon the Limits of Painting and Poetry,* tr. Ellen Frothingham (New York: Noonday, 1957), 91.

3. Ibid., 17.

4. Cf. John White, *The Birth and Rebirth of Pictorial Space* (New York: Harper and Row, 1972), 116.

5. Michael Fried, "Art and Objecthood," in *Minimal Art: A Critical Anthology,* ed. Gregory Battock (New York: Dutton, 1968), 145, n. 19.

6. Peter Eisenmann, "The End of the Classical: The End of the Beginning, The End of the End," *Perspecta* 21 (1984): 54.

7. Quoted by Fried in "Art and Objecthood," 144.

8. Fried, "Art and Objecthood," 144.

9. Karsten Harries, *The Bavarian Rococo Church: Between Faith and Aestheticism* (New Haven and London: Yale University Press, 1983), 86.

10. Heinrich Wölfflin, *Principles of Art History: The Problem of the Development of Style in Later Art,* tr. M. D. Hottinger (New York: Dover, n.d.), 63.

11. Ibid., 115.

12. Ibid., 115.

13. Ibid., 149

14. Robert Venturi, *Complexity and Contradiction in Architecture* (New York: Museum of Modern Art, 1977), especially the preface.

15. Wölfflin, *Principles of Art History,* 185.

16. Ibid.

17. Cf. the young Heidegger's understanding of "situation" as a temporal counterpart to what in *Being and Time* is discussed as "region." "Über das Wesen der Universität und des akademischen Studiums," Summer semester 1919, in Martin Heidegger, *Zur Bestimmung der Philosophie, Gesamtausgabe* vol. 56/57 (Frankfurt: Klostermann, 1987), 205–14.

18. Martin Heidegger, "Bauen Wohnen Denken," *Vorträge und Aufsätze* (Pfullingen: Neske, 1954), 161. Tr. A. Hofstadter, "Building Dwelling Thinking," in *Poetry, Language, Thought* (New York: Harper and Row, 1971), 160.

19. Martin Heidegger, "Die Gefahr," unpublished typescript, 25.

20. Ibid.

21. Mircea Eliade, *Cosmos and History: The Myth of the Eternal Return,* tr. Willard T.

Trask (New York: Harper Torchbooks, 1959), 151.

22. See Karsten Harries, "Building and the Terror of Time," *Perspecta* 19 (1979): 59–69.

23. Plato, *Philebus,* 51 c–d, tr. Benjamin Jowett.

24. Le Corbusier and Ozenfant, "Purism," *Modern Artists on Art,* ed. Robert L. Herbert (Englewood Cliffs: Prentice Hall, 1964), 60.

25. Ibid.

26. Quoted from an uncompleted manuscript, 1931, by Charles Jencks, in *Modern Movements in Architecture* (Garden City: Doubleday Anchor, 1973), 32–33.

27. Franz Kafka, "Der Bau," *Die Erzählungen* (Frankfurt: Fischer, 1961), 378–418. See Walter Biemel, *Philosophische Analysen zur Kunst der Gegenwart* (The Hague: Martinus Nijhoff, 1968).

28. René Descartes, *Discourse on the Method,* VI, tr. E. S. Haldane; and G. R. T. Ross, *The Philosophical Works* (New York: Dover, 1955), 1:119.

29. Friedrich Nietzsche, *Thus Spake Zarathustra,* Second Part, "On Redemption, " tr. Walter Kaufmann, *The Portable Nietzsche,* (Harmondsworth: Penguin Books, 1976), 251–52. Paraphrased by Martin Heidegger, *What Is Called Thinking?,* tr. J. Glen Gray (New York: Harper and Row, 1968), 103.

30. See Harries, *The Bavarian Rococo Church,* 156–75.

31. See Hans Sedlmayr, *Verlust der Mitte* (Berlin: Ulstein, 1959), 77.

32. Joseph Rykwert, *On Adam's House in Paradise: The Idea of the Primitive Hut in Architectural Theory* (New York: Museum of Modern Art, 1972).

33. Frank Lloyd Wright, *The Living City,* quoted by Rykwert, *On Adam's House in Paradise,* 17

34. Ibid., 17.

35. Ibid., 18.

36. Jencks, *Modern Movements in Architecture,* 273.

37. See Karsten Harries, "Modernity's Bad Conscience," *AA Files* 10 (1985): 53–60.

38. Jencks, *Modern Movements in Architecture,* 277.

39. Ibid.

40. Ibid., 291.

41. Quoted in Jencks, *Modern Movements in Architecture,* 295.

42. Quoted in Jencks, *Modern Movements in Architecture,* 297.

43. See Karsten Harries, "The Voices of Space," *Center* 4 (1988): 34–49.

44. Gaston Bachelard, *The Poetics of Space,* tr. Maria Jolas (Boston: Beacon Press, 1969), 7.

45. Ibid., 103.

Order and Change in Architecture 3
Christian Norberg-Schulz

Architects are not philosophers: nevertheless they have to expend thought on the nature of their field. Sometimes these thoughts determine practice, and sometimes they justify it. Often the justification of one architect becomes a guideline for others. In a few cases thought (not to say "theory") and practice go together, and become an authentic quest for *meaning*.

The word *meaning* is the key to the present situation. In its late, postwar phase, modern architecture had become meaningless, whether in the sense of sterile schematism or as arbitrary invention. It did not speak any more, and the built environment often lost its traditional identity. As a reaction against this state of affairs Sigfried Giedion, speaking for the modern movement, launched demands for a "new monumentality" and a "new regionalism." He defined monumentality as the expression of "the eternal need of people to create symbols for their activities and for their fate or destiny, for their religious beliefs and for their social convictions,"[1] and he intended regionalism as the "careful, reverent study of the way of life of the place," a study which ought to be taken as the point of departure for planning and building.[2] Both demands stemmed from the realization "that the rationalist and exclusively materialist attitude, upon which the latest phase of Western civilization has been grounded, is insufficient."[3] In terms of architectural theory, insufficiency implies in this case a rejection of Sullivan's slogan "Form Follows Function," which for some decades had served as the banner of modern architecture.

In reality, Sullivan's slogan had never been followed by the protagonists of modernism, who used it as a justification rather than a guiding principle. It was left to the epigones to base their work on this seemingly significant statement, without, however, arriving at *definition* of the three terms involved, especially the mysterious word "follows," which should somehow establish a link between human needs and actions on the one hand and the forms we choose for their satisfaction on the other.

Some thought was certainly given to the problem. For example, Le Corbusier's "Five Points towards a New Architecture" are well known, and were intended to serve as a generally valid "grammar" of design.[4] Beyond their possible utility, Le Corbusier's points are interesting because they represent the wish for a return to the beginning, defining the basic modes of a building's being in space: that is, its way of standing on the ground (*pilotis*), receiving the sky (*toits-jardins*), extending horizontally (*plan libre*), and relating to the environment through opening and closure (*fenêtre en longueur, facade libre*). Similarly Giedion wrote that "we had to begin anew, . . . as if nothing had ever been done before."[5] All the same, the dimensions of monumentality and regionalism are left out, since Le Corbusier's points implied solutions of an abstract, "place-free" character. Le Corbusier himself must have realized their insufficiency when he began to design the pilgrimage chapel at Ronchamp in 1950. Here he defined the task as construction of a "vessel of intense concentration and meditation,"[6] and the principles of modern architecture therefore had to be superseded by a new approach. Le Corbusier wrote that when he visited the building site for the first time in June, 1950, he spent three hours there "to get acquainted with the ground and the horizons."[7] Hence the design expresses the wish to relate an introverted "vessel of meditation" to the surrounding landscape, and modern architecture—perhaps for the first time—has accepted the challenge of creating a *place* where life may be conducted.

Ronchamp initiated a more comprehensive approach to architecture, but it did not offer a new general basis upon which to build. As a unique solution, it did not possess the *typological* value of the early Christian basilica, the Gothic cathedral, or the Palladian villa, and those who tried to imitate its forms failed utterly. Nonetheless the comprehensive attitude survived, and a valid new approach is certainly more important than the imitation of any model. In general, Le Corbusier's patient search may be understood as the wish to unite order and change, or in other words to relate the new, dynamic world of modern times to what he called "the laws of the sun and the site."[8]

Several younger architects understood the message and tried to arrive at principles of general validity based on the realization that architecture primarily means the creation of *places,* rather than the mere satisfaction of "functions." Especially interesting is the contribution of Danish architect Jorn Utzon, who, with his concept of platform and hovering roof, gave the *plan libre* a new concrete identity between earth and sky.[9] Furthermore I may mention the Finn Reima Pietilä, who started developing ideas for his student union building *Dipoli* in Otaniemi by "walking, zigzagging across the shield rock of the building site, achieving a tactile memory of the understanding of the rock form." Thus he obtained what he calls a "pre-cognitive knowledge" of the site, "in contrast to scientific methods," and *Dipoli* became "a composition where nature is the creative artist and the sylvan genius loci its theme."[10] Pietilä's approach evidently reaches beyond a general sense of space, and really aims at grasping what *is there,* as objects of human identification: trees, rocks, clouds, and light.[11] Utzon and Pietilä are Nordic architects, and in fact the new regionalism originated in Finland, especially in the works of Alvar Aalto.[12] However, we find a related approach in southern Europe, and I may mention as the most significant example the school of Ticino and Mario Botta; Botta has pointed repeatedly to the regional roots of his buildings. The works of Utzon, Pietilä, and Botta undoubtedly represent an important step towards a more authentic architecture, and again we encounter the wish to found modernism on an order inherent in nature. In addition, Botta introduces themes which appear in the guise of varied types in most of his buildings.

The need for typological forms was pointed out almost simultaneously by the Italian Aldo Rossi and the American Robert Venturi, who in spite of their differences have in common the aim of creating a generally understood architecture.[13] I cannot discuss their ideas here, but mention them to emphasize that, during the 1960s, the quest for meaning became of general concern. Rossi and Venturi are not explicitly referring to regionalism, but in their works they certainly represent Italian and American traditions, respectively. Both are deeply concerned with the problems of modern society, Rossi from a radical political point of view, and Venturi on the basis of a desire to express the complexities of modern experience. Thus, we encounter once more the wish to cope with change *and* order. Many more names could be mentioned in this context, but I shall restrict myself to discussing the ideas of the most important exponent of comprehensive modernism, Louis Kahn.

Kahn also took the modernist demand for a return to beginnings as his point of departure, but he did not reduce this concept to what is measurable, that is, to a rational understanding of function and form. Rather he asked what a building "wants to be," suggesting that any work of architecture possesses an essence or general "form," which determined the solution.[14] The essence resides in the "beginning," when humanity came to realize "inspirations" and "desires" and "institutions." What Kahn evidently has in mind here are basic human modes of being-in-the-world, or *Dasein,* to use a term from Heidegger. Life is not arbitrary, but has a structure which comprises both humankind and nature. "It is not what you want, but what you sense in the order of things which tells you what to design." Hence, the individual work of architecture becomes "an offering to Architecture," with a capital A. Kahn relates the word "inspiration" to light as the symbol of understanding and the "giver of all presences."[15]

Kahn does not explicitly refer to demands for meaning and regional roots, but he certainly implies these aims in his distinction between what is "general" and what is "circumstantial," and in his definition of the single work as a "world within a world."[16] Particularly important is his notion of basic forms (fig. 3.1). It implies that he no longer accepts that the solution "follows" from the functions, but returns to the ancient acknowledgment that any solution presupposes a given lan-

Fig. 3.1. Louis Kahn —Convent for the Dominican Sisters, Media, Pennsylvania. Project, 1965.

guage for its realization. The word *follows* is hence interpreted as a *means,* in the true sense of something that mediates and establishes a meaning. We understand that in Kahn's thinking the intuitions of Le Corbusier and the younger architects mentioned above are implicitly present, and that his philosophy rescues architecture from relativism, by coping with order as well as change.

Kahn's qualitative approach to architecture made a deep impression when it came forth towards the end of the 1950s.[17] Since he stated his ideas in an aphoristic form rather than as a coherent way of thought, however, they need further elaboration to become a point of departure for present-day practice. In my opinion, the necessary clarification is offered by the thinking of Martin Heidegger.

Several years ago, when I read Heidegger's essays on "Building Dwelling Think-

46

ing" and "The Thing," I was struck by the similarity between his thoughts and those of Louis Kahn, and realized that the fragmentary and somewhat obscure philosophy of the latter could be developed into a true theory of architecture with the aid of Heidegger's professional and systematic investigations.[18] Although Heidegger takes care to say that he does not pretend to "discover architectural ideas" or "give rules for building,"[19] the references to architecture in his writings are numerous, and the very concept of *dwelling* is of central importance. Thus he says that "dwelling is the manner in which mortals are on earth."[20] Evidently dwelling is the general purpose of architecture, and the modern movement explicitly took the creation of a "new dwelling" as its point of departure.[21]

To clarify Heidegger's concept of dwelling, I shall turn to one of his less familiar essays, the beautiful *Hebel der Hausfreund.* Here we read, "The buildings bring the earth as the inhabited landscape close to man and at the same time place the nearness of neighborly dwelling under the expanse of the sky" (fig. 3.2).[22] In the text Heidegger also states that the word *buildings* refers to single houses as well as villages and cities. Moreover he says that the buildings in and about themselves "gather" the "world" that is inhabited by man. The word *landscape* therefore implies something more than a given, natural place; rather it means that "multifarious between," says Heidegger, "where man accomplishes his wandering from birth to death between earth and sky." The buildings "admit" this accomplishment if they are "tuned" to dwelling. The world as the "multifarious between" is the "house" where man dwells, and it is "gathered" and "expressed" by the poet or, in our context, by the builder or architect. Hence dwelling is in truth "poetical."[23]

To clarify the quotation from *Hebel der Hausfreund,* certain explanations are necessary. First of all Heidegger tells us that a work of architecture serves "to bring the inhabited landscape close to man." An inhabited landscape is a place between earth and sky where human life takes place. As earth and sky, it comprises all natural phenomena, as indicated in Heidegger's essays "Building Dwelling Thinking" and "The Thing."[24] When these phenomena gather to form a distinct totality or "thing," we speak of a "landscape" or "region" (*Gegend*), and the very names given to these entities express their nature: island, valley, basin, plain. Sometimes the individual landscape may get its name from particular features, as in the case of the Black Forest or the Rocky Mountains.

That the landscape is "inhabited" means that it is recognized as such, understood, and cultivated. People thus act as the "guardians" of what is present, and through cultivation reveal the essence of the place. Among the means used to this end, buildings are of prime importance, because they bring the inhabited landscape close. This implies that it is not enough to recognize the landscape as such; it also has to be kept and expressed in images that *reveal* and *endure.* Heidegger uses the bridge to illustrate this point (fig. 3.3), saying: "The bridge . . . does not

Fig. 3.2. "The buildings bring the earth . . ." —a Black Forest farmhouse.

just connect banks that are already there. The banks emerge as banks only as the bridge crosses the stream. . . . With the banks, the bridge brings to the stream the one and the other expanse of the landscape lying behind them. It brings stream and bank and land into each other's neighborhood. The bridge *gathers* the earth as landscape around the stream."[25] Thus the bridge relates the human actions that it serves to the given environment, and an "inhabited landscape" emerges. Houses, villages, and cities do the same, and thus they express *Dasein* as poetical dwelling.

Evidently this is accomplished in a twofold way. First, "gathering" means that a *Gegend* or space is defined where life may occur. I have used the word *admittance* in this connection, a word that corresponds to Heidegger's *einräumen,* which literally means "give space to" (fig. 3.4).[26] Through the clearing of a space

Fig. 3.3. "The bridge does not just . . ."— Roman bridge in Ticino.

(*räumen*), life is admitted (*eingeräumt*). According to Heidegger the result is a place (*Ort*), which as a region gathers the things that belong together.[27] Second, therefore, "gathering" means the bringing together of *some-thing*. That is, a place is not a mere space, but is constituted by the very things that it gathers. Again I shall refer to names to illustrate this fact. "Valley" comes from the Latin *vallis,* which is derived from *vallum,* wall or mound. Accordingly Heidegger says, "A boundary is not that at which something stops, but, as the Greeks recognized, the boundary is that from which something begins its presencing."[28] A boundary or wall is certainly a concrete thing, and as such it "gathers a world." The very word *thing* in fact means gathering,[29] and therefore the thing "visits mortals with a world."[30] Its meaning consists in what it gathers, that is, in its relations to other things, and hence Heidegger understands the world as a "mirror-play" of things: earth and sky, divinities and mortals.[31] Gathering thus depends not only on ad-

Fig. 3.4. "Einräumen"
—Monteriggioni near
Siena.

mittance, but also positively on what Heidegger calls "thinging."

As things, buildings bring an inhabited landscape close to us. They do this by standing forth in the open as concrete identities, and their meaning is embodied in their *Gestalt*.[32] Heidegger explains this property of buildings in his essay "The Origin of the Work of Art," using a Greek temple as his example.[33] He begins by emphasizing that a building "portrays nothing." Evidently, it cannot therefore be understood fully as a sign or symbol, but rather is a "new" thing that "simply stands there in the rock-cleft valley." Four times Heidegger repeats that the temple acts as it does by *standing there*. By standing there it reveals the properties of the earth and the things and beings that inhabit the earth. Thus it opens up a world, "giving to things their look and to men their outlook on themselves." Heidegger,

however, only suggests *how* this is accomplished, saying for instance that "the luster and gleam of the stone . . . first brings to light the light of day, the breadth of the sky, the darkness of the night." The act of standing and the quality of material are aspects of embodiment which, together with other properties, make up a figure or *Gestalt*.[34] In this essay Heidegger defines embodiment as a "setting back into the earth," whereas in the later essay "Die Kunst und der Raum," he preferred the simpler term *Verkörperung* (fig. 3.5).[35] Plastic form thus is defined as "the embodiment of a place that opens up a region," and its content includes the "characters that constitute the place."[36] To conclude, he sums up his thought on *Verkörperung* in the phrase: "Plastic form: the embodiment of the truth of Being in the work that founds its place."[37]

Fig. 3.5. "Verköperung" —Stonehenge, Salisbury Plain.

Heidegger's thinking on architecture as such breaks off here, but nevertheless it offers necessary clarification, since it organizes and explains the intuitions of the architects mentioned above. The concept of embodiment thus is implied in the motto used by Le Corbusier as a heading to each of the three theoretical chapters in his early book *Vers une architecture.* There we read:

> You employ stone, wood and concrete, and with these materials you build houses and palaces. That is *construction.* Ingenuity is at work. But suddenly you touch my heart, you do me good, I am happy and I say: 'This is beautiful.' That is architecture. Art enters in. My house is practical. I thank you, as I might thank Railway engineers, or the Telephone service. You have not touched my heart. But suppose that walls rise towards heaven in such a way that I am moved. I perceive your intentions. Your mood has been gentle, brutal, charming or noble. The stones you have erected tell me so. You fix me to the place and my eyes regard it. They behold something which expresses a thought. A thought which reveals itself without word or sound, but solely by means of shapes which stand in a certain relationship to one another. These shapes are such that they are clearly revealed in light. The relationships between them have not necessarily any reference to what is practical or descriptive. They are the language of Architecture. By the use of raw materials and starting from conditions more or less utilitarian, you have established certain relationships which have aroused my emotions. This is *Architecture.*[38]

In this statement, Le Corbusier explicitly proceeds beyond functionalism, talking as Heidegger does about the meaning expressed by a building's standing there, or rather its rising towards heaven, (fig. 3.6) and even calling the relationships in question the "language of Architecture."

Heidegger's concept of the world as between earth and sky is paralleled by Utzon's platforms and hovering roofs, and his poetic understanding of landscape is echoed in Pietilä's notion of pre-cognitive knowledge. Kahn's love of beginnings is related to Heidegger's concept of *Anfang,* which he presents in *Grundfragen der Philosophie,* saying: "In the beginning everything is decided."[39] Evidently here he comes close to Kahn's dictum: "What will be has always been." Finally, Heidegger's notion of *Lichtung,* that is, "clearing" or "lightening,"[40] corresponds to Kahn's definition of light as "the giver of all presences." Before I discuss the implied problem of order and change, however, I must consider Heidegger's most important contribution to our understanding: the notion of architecture as *language.*

To regard architecture as a number "language" is certainly nothing new. The styles of the past were indeed languages; they were given in advance as a body of interrelated forms, and hence enabled the architect to express a circumstantial situation as part of a world. When modernism abolished styles a vacuum was

Fig. 3.6. "Standing there . . ."—Hera temples, Paestum.

created which the modernists hoped, rather optimistically, to fill, with the aid of the idea that form follows function. The history of modern architecture shows that this hope has not been fullfilled.

As a consequence of the failure of functionalism, the problem of language has come to the fore, but so far it has mainly been approached in terms of semiology; any architectural form is viewed as a sign that carries a meaning in agreement with an established code. In general architecture is understood as a communication of such meanings; that is, any form "communicates the function to be fulfilled."[41] Thus Umberto Eco says that a stair is a sign that "denotes the possibility of going up."[42] If we return to Heidegger's example, a bridge would then be a sign that denotes the possibility of crossing the river! It certainly is, but Heidegger has shown that it is also something *more:* as a gathering thing it brings an inhab-

53

ited landscape close to us and opens up a world. Therefore, to quote Gadamer, it "presents an increase in the being."[43] In other words, it is a "new" thing, the meaning of which consists in the world it gathers. It is not a symbol either, because a symbol represents something that is present elsewhere.[44] It follows that a work of architecture cannot be explained as simply a sign; semiological interpretations are therefore as a rule somewhat pedestrian.

Heidegger's conception of language is entirely different. He does not understand language primarily as communication or information, but as the "House and Being," that is, as the abode where the nature or essence of things is kept and revealed. "In the naming, the things named are called into their thinging," Heidegger says, and "thinging they unfold world, in which things abide."[45] Therefore *language speaks,* and "man speaks only as he responds to language."[46] This conception of language may of course be refuted on the assumption that the content of words undergoes a continuous process of change, or that they mean something different to me than to you. Heidegger emphasizes, however, that we would not be able to recognize any thing if we did not in advance "possess" its essence. Thus he says, "'House' is in contrast to the single house, *what already was,*" and "houseness is not perceived, and still it remains in an eminent sense in view: it is 'seen' in advance."[47] Here we remember Kahn's "what . . . has always been" and also realize the truth of a much more famous statement: "In the beginning was the Word."

What, then, is the essence that comes into "thinging" in the naming? To the Greeks, it was the *eidos,* the *look* of a thing, that stands forth into the open (fig. 3.7). Thus we know "fish" and "fowl," and when something escapes our recognition we say that it is "neither fish nor fowl." This seemingly banal fact is of fundamental importance, because it confirms that thing and *Gestalt* belong together.[48] In the poetical saying of language the structure or articulation of the *Gestalt* is revealed, and thus it becomes part of an understood world. A saying of this kind presupposes an attitude of *Erstaunen* or "wonder."[49] It has to be emphasized, however, that when something is revealed as something, other aspects of the things are simultaneously concealed. If that were not the case, revelation would soon be complete, and history come to an end.[50]

How does this understanding of language relate to architecture? Although poetry is the original art, it does not exhaust the disclosure of truth. In poetic language truth is brought "to word." But it also has to be "set-into-work." Human life takes place between earth and sky in a concrete sense, and the things which constitute the place have to be revealed in their immediate presence. It is this kind of disclosure that is accomplished by the Greek temple. Thus Heidegger says that man dwells "between work and word."[51] The word opens up the world, the work gives it concrete presence. This disclosure is only possible if architecture is a "language." As a language, Architecture, with a capital A, is the "House of Man's

Fig. 3.7. Eidos—The atelier of Constantin Brancusi, Paris.

Being in between Earth and Sky." And as such it contains the basic structures of allowance and embodiment, as well as their synthesis in nameable *Gestalten,* or typological entities. We could also say that it comprises the "where, how, and what" of man's spatial *Dasein.*

It is already implied in Heidegger's terms *Einraumen* and *Verkörperung* that the "where" and the "how" refer to the architectural dimensions of spatial organization and built form, respectively. Whereas the former has been well elucidated during the last decades in connection with studies of human environmental orientation,[52] the latter is still a problem to be explored. How do we *identify* with the standing, rising, opening, and closing of a built form, and how do these properties determine the character of a place? I have offered a first approximation to the problem in my book *The Concept of Dwelling,*[53] but a systematic phenomenological investigation has yet to be done. Evidently embodiment is intimately connected with building in the sense of *techné;* that is, the making of gathering things. Heidegger points out that to the Greeks *techné* means to make something appear as what it *is,* and that the tectonics of architecture ought to preserve this original meaning.[54]

And finally, the "what" of the language of architecture has hardly been considered at all. It is Leon Krier's great merit to have reminded us of the fact that architecture primarily consists of "nameable objects," and that the alienation of modern architecture stems from the oblivion of the concrete *Gestalten* that possess a name, such as a tower, gable, arch, or dome. We remember Heidegger's assertion that the object of man's wonder is the *eidos* of things, and may also recall the question in Rilke's "Ninth Elegy": "Are we perhaps *here* to say: house, bridge, fountain, gate, jug, fruit tree, window—at best: column, tower . . . ?" The nameable objects evidently constitute the content of human *memory,* and Heidegger explicitly states: "Memory is the source of poetry."[55] Again he refers to the Greeks, whose goddess Mnemosyne, or memory, was the mother of Muses, with Zeus as the father. Zeus needed memory to bring forth art, and Mnemosyne herself was the daughter of earth and sky.

Summing up, I may assert that Heidegger's thinking offers the necessary point of departure for our understanding of the language of architecture: an understanding in which the dimensions of topology, morphology, and typology correspond to the aspects of where, how, and what. By means of the language of architecture, we are enabled to say "house," "gate," "window," and "tower" in a meaningful way, illuminating the present as the manifestation of something essential. Thus we not only bring the inhabited landscape close to us, but also place the nearness of neighborly dwelling under the expanse of the sky.

An authentic understanding of the language of architecture clarifies the problem of order and change. What remains the same, what has "always been," is not

The Voice of Architecture

4

First International Cubit Symposium on Architecture and Culture
Texas A&M University, College Station, Texas, April 13, 1989.
Panel discussion following invited papers.
Participants: Kenneth Frampton; Karsten Harries; Christian Norberg-Schulz.

Harries: In his lecture, Professor Norberg-Schulz suggested that we could fill in theoretically some thoughts we find, let us say, in Louis Kahn, by referring to a more rigorous treatment of these ideas in Heidegger. Let me refer to the famous temple passage in "The Origin of the Work of Art" where Heidegger speaks of the temple-work as establishing a world and presenting the earth.

Heidegger's example suggests a possibility for architecture as possessing a strong ethical function, giving us a coherent world understanding and placing us firmly on the earth. In context Heidegger makes it quite clear that such temple-work lies behind us. It belongs to a past from which we are separated, not only by the obvious years, but more importantly by the shape of our modern world. So the question is, can this kind of work, moving as it is, illuminate our practice today any more than, let's say, my examples of farmhouses or Heidegger's Black Forest farmhouse?

Norberg-Schulz: Heidegger's philosophy is truly dynamic: his return is not a return but, as he says, a second beginning. But he does not say that we start from zero. We start by guarding, by taking care of what we understood in the first beginning. Therefore, in my opinion, he is the only thinker who has managed to solve this riddle of constancy and change. "Constancy" is perhaps too strong a word; therefore I called my paper "Order and Change."

Heidegger does not mean that we should return to the Greek temple as such. He says in the text that "a building arises" first, and then a Greek temple. That is, a Greek temple is an example of a certain *kind* of building, but he says "a building." What he talks about doesn't lie behind us. He tries to arrive at what he calls "the same," *das Selb,* which is always there but needs ever-new interpretations. I used that tomb by Carlo Scarpa to show that these basic recognitions

Fig. 4.1. Constancy and Change 1. © Richard Payne AIA 1989

or understandings need ever-new interpretations, and yet when we interpret something in a new way we hide something which the Greeks may have revealed. Still, we are within the same basic framework of things. That, I think, is important, because otherwise we will really remain with relativism, or actually nihilism.

Of course I agree that there are many reasons to be pessimistic today. When Heidegger asks, "Is it possible to do things in this way in our time?" then it is very tempting to say no. Well, personally I am an optimist, and that may be why I say yes. But I think it is actually very simple. I have seen with many architecture students that if you put them on a certain track, suddenly they are there and do it. So it is not that difficult. And I think every child shows that one returns "to the things themselves" over and over again. Children start with these basic recognitions, these beginnings or *Anfangen*. Therefore I think we might arrive at a better understanding of things and of architecture if we introduced something like environmental training or education as early as in the primary schools.

Harries: I think we are both optimists, and I think we also basically agree about where we want to end up. We also agree that Heidegger is useful in this discussion, but I think where the difference lies is that we disagree about the exact nature of that usefulness. In "The Origin of the Work of Art" Heidegger concludes with a postscript citing Hegel's famous words, "Art in its highest sense lies behind us." Art able to establish a world — art in that sense which Heidegger really wants to return to — he calls "rendered into question" by developments that have taken place. Heidegger then adds, "The truth of Hegel's judgment has not been decided." So he concludes with a real question mark. He himself is not convinced by the relevance of his own example — the Black Forest example — to the modern world.

When we talk about "the thing," as in Professor Norberg-Schulz's essay, Heidegger's full understanding of "the thing" has to be fleshed out in terms of the fourfold of earth and sky, mortals and divinities. We all know how hard it is for us to make sense of that fourfold. We have little trouble with earth and sky; we can talk about the colonnade as representing people; mortals are easy too. But we have the biggest trouble with divinities. What in the world do we moderns mean when we speak of "divinities"? How can we fill that in? Many of us can't. From Heidegger's point of view, "the thing" in its full sense is something that we are shut off from; access to it is denied to us.

In these passages, Heidegger talks about "our world" as being a deficient world; he calls it *die verwahrlose Welt. Verwahrlos* means the world which has sort of gone to pot, has lost its measure. Heidegger has an understanding of history, of the history of Being which culminates in technology, which makes optimism very, very difficult. In countless essays Heidegger has developed an understanding of history which makes it terribly difficult to use Heidegger in the kind of program which I think both Professor Norberg-Schulz and I want to support. In order to carry that program off, I think we can't use Heidegger without also subjecting him to a profound critique, and that is, I think, the first difference here between us.

Norberg-Schulz: Well, Heidegger unfortunately—or maybe fortunately—continues to publish after his death. [*Laughter*] Yes, I just received volume sixty-five of his collected works the other day. He held it back for many years, considering it one of his most important works. But, he said, before you read that you have to read all my lectures, because if not you will not understand it. Finally now the lectures are published, in about thirty volumes, and when you have read all that, then you can read volume sixty-five, and then wait for volumes sixty-six, sixty-seven, up to about volume eighty, and I will be dead, I think, when they are out. [*Laughter*] So to judge the use of Heidegger along with Karsten is something I don't dare to do, because his work is not yet clear to us. That volume sixty-five is extremely important, and very difficult, too. I wouldn't consider it a pessimistic volume, but it is not easy. Therefore I don't think it is interesting to discuss whether Heidegger was pessimistic or not.

In Heidegger's essay "Do We Need Poets in a Destitute Time?" he refers to Rilke. He was obviously, I think, a little jealous of Rilke, because Rilke says many of the same things in a much better way. He was a real poet, and he says things very beautifully. So Heidegger tries to reduce Rilke a bit, and says, well, he was a poet, but in a destitute time. He concludes that we need these people, but there are hardly any more left. That, of course, would make us pessimistic again. But I think poets will come forth again; why shouldn't they?

Heidegger refers to Hegel and says that great art is behind us. If it is conceived as an art which wants to embrace everything, a total, unified, harmonious system comprising everything, I don't think we can return to that. In today's pluralistic world we have to make choices much more than before. We choose different types of theses about our "being in the world," and I don't want to prevent other people from making a different choice from me—choices, usually about divinities. To many people this is not a problem, but a choice. Lots of young people become Buddhists today. And therefore the fourfold of Heidegger seems to be a kind of need to many people still. His thinking opens our eyes to very important issues of human existence, not only dwelling, but also this wider issue of the mirror-play of things, of the fourfold.

Anyhow, in my reading Heidegger is not so pessimistic. In one of his most beautiful small texts he says, "We are too late for the gods, and too early for Being. Being's poem is man." Too late for the comprehensive answers of the gods, and too early for the realization of the person which Karsten also talked about today. We are too late and too early, so we live in a very difficult time. Let us look at the future as the possibility of then realizing that poem which is humanity.

Harries: Well, again we agree on the essentials. The very statement you just quoted, "We are too late for the gods," also entails, "We are too late for works like the Greek temple." Now, Heidegger also says, "All my thinking can only be understood in relation to Hölderlin." For him Hölderlin is the poet who changes the map of poetry, of art. With that something new happens. From now on, in this modern destitute time, according to Heidegger, art is simply not able to do

Fig. 4.2. Constancy and Change 2. © Richard Payne AIA 1989

what the Greek temple could do. We have to be content with a much more modest role for art, which can perhaps recall us to the earth, make us listen more carefully. But the great syntheses establish a world: an order in which things and persons find their place, a world in which to stand in the world is to know what is to be done. In that sense, Heidegger suggests, art is no longer possible for us. Nor will there be architecture able to do that. The Gothic cathedral and the Greek temple were works in that sense, but no modern work of architecture can be. Something has changed the significance of art and architecture, which Heidegger correctly links to the rise of technological industrial society, including capitalism. Art means less to us, has become more peripheral, than it was, let's say, in the Gothic period when you couldn't even distinguish between art and religion.

To use Heidegger, then, we must take very seriously his understanding of the modern period as the technological age. One lesson we have to learn from Heidegger is the question: "What is it to build? What is it to create architecture in a technological age—without saying no to technology?"

Norberg-Schulz: I'm not sure what you mean by art "in that sense." Do you refer to art as something that represents a total world? These total worlds in the past were within only one world although there were many such; you also had cultures in China and Japan and so on. What is happening today is not that these worlds necessarily belong to the past, but that they are mixed together and come together in a new state of pluralism. The result is that we are now subject to choice and not automatically part of such a system. But it is still there, and we can make a choice. And we can express that choice still in architecture.

I think architecture will do exactly the same today as it did before, and I used Scarpa's tomb to show that. It doesn't look like a Greek temple, but it works basically in the same way. What we ought to learn today, and what we need as a result of our choice, is to create not a total embracing system, but what I have called in an essay on American architecture "islands of meaning" representing these various choices.

On the question of technology today, I agree with Ken that all architecture forms a technological basis. I don't think you can invent any form which is not related somehow to building, to making. Think about the elements of architecture as they were known in the past—the column, the beam, the arch, the vault, the dome: they are all the technological basis. That basis should also be respected today.

But in the past, at least, these forms tended to liberate themselves somehow from that direct technological reference. They became what, in my first book, *Intentions in Architecture,* I called "fictitious construction." In the Renaissance the best architects—Brunelleschi or Michelangelo—dressed up their buildings with pilasters and architraves which simulated a structure but indeed were not a structure at all. But of course they did refer back to a real structure. However they were not just signs of that structure, in a kind of semiological sense; they were much more. They represented a structure in which the walls, in Heidegger's sense, were a thing again.

So I think that we cannot just deny that such fictitious structures might be an alternative to real structures in certain contexts. The decorated shed is not the only solution to architecture, certainly not. Maybe it should even be an exception. But here and there it might be quite a good alternative, as shown by Karsten's peasant house in Bavaria, which was rather beautiful, I think, although it was really a decorated shed.

This question of technology is really important, and complex. I studied with Pier-Luigi Nervi myself, and learned about reinforced concrete and how to express forces. But he also said that they were very lucky at the turn of the century when they still had the language of forms at their disposal.

Frampton: You know, in some ways there is quite a strong tendency to avoid the political. To the extent that I think of myself as having a political position, this position emerged out of being an architect first, then coming to the United States, and strangely enough being politicized by the experience in the United States. When we start with the P's—with political or pessimism and pluralism—we could add to it also Prometheanism.

One of the problems with modern pluralism is that, though we like to talk about choices, and think that we do make choices, what is strange is how little choice there really is. A lot of the choices in modern society are, in fact, very trivial choices. The market lives on the myth of choice, but corporations and large industrial organizations actually arrange things so that there isn't as much choice as one might like to think.

In this regard I am reminded of critical efforts made by architects, who had rather a strong grip of reality and a certain modesty, to propose alternative land settlement patterns for late-capitalist society. Such land settlement patterns would minimize the consumption of land, and were by that token technologically oriented. Those land settlement patterns have never been put into action as a real norm, and that raises very serious questions as to why not. What are the factors in government that have mitigated against such land settlement patterns? I am thinking of Chermayeff and Alexander's *Community and Privacy,* for example, and—less well known—of Roland Reiner's *Liveable Environments* which appeared almost a decade later. *Community and Privacy* was published twenty-five years ago. So actually fewer choices are available than one might imagine, I think. And this is one of the disturbing aspects of *die verwahrlose Welt* of Heidegger.

Somewhere Luis Barragan says, "An architecture that does not achieve serenity is an error." I think that is a remarkable critical statement. It is also a very modest statement, to accept the idea that architecture might be just a setting for life rather than the pre-emptive operation which, in our competitive society, it so often is. Because today of course if you don't compete, how will anyone ever notice you?

Vis-à-vis pessimism, one of the big problems of the West, and one of the problems that the West hates to face, is the western tradition of violence toward nature, an attitude that it is possible to dominate nature as opposed to having a symbiotic relationship with nature. I think this is the key, in a way, to the West's dilemma. The Orient has at least another tradition in its attitude towards nature and culture.

Finally, just one remark about pessimism. Somewhere Gramschi says, "The old is dying, and the new cannot be born, and in this interregnum, many morbid symptoms appear." In another passage, he speaks of the pessimism of the intelligence and the optimism of the will. I think that it isn't perhaps sufficient for the children of the Enlightenment to be told something as sobering as that. But maybe that's all we can be told.

Harries: I would like to turn now to the problem of language. For example, Venturi's decorated shed is not really just a shed with ornament added, a pretty pattern like a wallpaper pattern glued on a wall. What Venturi is after, and makes no bones about, is that he wants to return a linguistic element to architecture. He wants to add elements that in some sense will speak. He wants significations; he wants signs. But what the struggle is really about is to return to architecture something like a voice. You find, for example, in Tafuri's writings a recurring complaint that architecture has lost its voice. As a symptom, surely, that struggle must be taken very seriously, and we ought to think about what it is a symptom of, before we try to address whatever problem lies there. But there is a problem that is widely felt, not only by architects, but by the community at large. Why is there that concern about language?—which I take it is simply a fact.

Norberg-Schulz: I think that Ken Frampton is right in saying that in the West we always wanted to dominate nature. And if I understood you correctly that has led us astray, not to say into a rather dangerous crisis. And this is certainly also a political problem.

I say "also" because I think it is a lack of what we could call environmental awareness. I am not sure that we can turn around that unfortunate use of technologies today, just by political means. I think politics is usually very superficial. People vote for this precedent or that one, basically superficially even though it concerns all of us. Instead, if we would develop our environmental awareness, starting with the children, then maybe we would stop dominating nature in that unfortunate way. However, one could add that even in the eastern cultures which did not want to dominate nature, they are doing it all the same; it is going rather badly both in China and Japan. There, obviously, this awareness has also got lost.

That goes together, perhaps, with the question of language: what we do no longer has a relationship to the things themselves. What Frampton said this morning is very basic: we have to return to what you called an architecture of heaviness—not only that, but that is one aspect. We have to make something that really "stands there," as I tried to say also. We must try again to understand that

Fig. 4.3. Constancy and Change 3. © Richard Payne AIA 1989

Fig. 4.4. Constancy and Change 4. © Richard Payne AIA 1989

the expression of architecture resides in its standing on the ground and rising up in space and expanding horizontally. These are basic facts which are common to all civilizations, but which are used differently and which may even be negated, as the Gothic negated the classical way of standing. But in a certain sense the Gothic had to understand this language, to negate it. And it had to almost accept it to transform what was bodily presence into what was a line of force. Whereas in, say, Islamic architecture, these lines are no longer lines of force, but rather rays of light.

Why the question of language has come out is, I think, first of all due to the abstract attitude toward everything which has grown more and more prevalent since the Enlightenment. To quote Kahn again, we have really been interested only in what is measurable. Language is, instead, by its nature not measurable. It is poetical, Heidegger tells us, and not he alone. And that has somehow been forgotten. I think that is probably the reason language has gotten into a crisis. Therefore instead of using language we have tended to make functional diagrams and then build them. So I see the talks today—Frampton's insistence on making, insistence on tectonics—as a very important aspect of returning to the things themselves. And I think that is part of the return to language.

Harries: I agree with you. I wonder whether you would use this formulation: I think one aspect of the language crisis in architecture today is that language—in a narrow sense, as words written down or spoken—has been taken too seriously. Our culture is in this sense linguistic. Stories, in that quite literal sense, play an important part in the leading styles. If you look at the Gothic style as a symbol system, that depends heavily on a verbal component which for the most part no longer convinces us today. That vocabulary lies behind us. It is a matter for art historians to write up—let's say, Otto von Simpson in his book on the Gothic cathedral. The Bavarian Rococo church—again, a very developed symbol system—establishes a world into which we cannot step back. It too lies behind us.

When we look at the great styles of the past, we have an amalgam of elements which still speak to us: pediments, columns, the way a building rests on the ground. But we have lost a lot of the symbolism that particular architectural elements carry. For example, the column had also a political significance. The fact that the column proliferated in the vernacular of this country as perhaps nowhere else is, I think, not an innocent fact.

So we have symbol systems which have decayed in the sense that the worldview that supported them is no longer shared, but I don't think that means that there is nothing in this architecture which speaks today. A great deal still speaks to us.

I think the mistake of many Postmodernists has been to furnish us with something like metasymbols. They take, let's say, the keystone, isolate it, and throw it around as an element. Let's give Graves credit for that: since his keystones, I have suddenly noticed how many keystones there are in the American vernacular. I'm grateful to him for that. I have seen keystones where I'd never seen

5

The Modern City:
Context, Site, or Place for Architecture?
Alberto Perez-Gomez

The difficulty modern architects, preservation specialists, and planners have with the question of context and "place" is the direct result of what we must characterize as a typically modern cultural dilemma. By this I mean the challenge of imagining and building a meaningful human order in a world which is still in the grip of the dualistic mentality of Descartes, and in which "reality" and delusions of Baconian "progress" are still strongly fueled today by the apparent successes of technology in controlling and dominating the environment. In this predominantly scientistic world, what gets built reflects little else but the enshrined, supposedly objective (and at best hedonistic) values of economy and efficiency that instantiate monetary or political power. While inhabiting such a world, professionals and clients alike also realize that the perceived order of our cities is radically impoverished by comparison to the richness and imagery of preindustrial and traditional urban counterparts.

The so-called debate about context is easily trivialized by architects and the public if we do not question certain deep-rooted assumptions. First of all, if the problem of architecture is understood in a purely formal sense, then the issue of what belongs in a site, or what is appropriate, can never be resolved. The ultimate relativity of value is insurmountable, if architecture is reduced to a question of esthetics (in the eighteenth-century sense), or "ornament" (in the nineteenth-century sense). If we accept the question of origin or ground as a metaphysical prejudice and remain content to dismiss the problem, we reduce architecture to form and end up with architecture as text and con-text. The end. Of the "classical" and everything else.[1]

Through our discussion of context and place in this article, other options will appear. Both positions, whether against or for contextualism, are equally fallacious if one understands context as a materialistic, dead, and objectified "formal" collection of buildings and physical features. Such a "context" can never be the origin for the generation of meaningful architectural ideas and built work. The desire to relate recent urban architecture to our historical tradition, as a reaction to the banality of technological modernism, is a noble objective. Context as a lifeless form in the sense sketched above, however, is far from being a synonym for history.

To grasp the significance of history as the true ground of architecture, we must see it as a narrative leading to our self-understanding as modern architects, and to a definition of what it is appropriate for us to do, here and now. History, in this sense, will be conducive to a *praxis* as a true embodiment of our *theoria*. Authentic history is never simply given like the objective "context"; we have to make it at every moment. We weave it in the present through our own desire. Because history is authentic knowledge (and not scientisitic pseudoknowledge or information), it demands that we take a position. History is our full inheritance, the western and European tradition of architectural artifacts which are our symbols because *we* have made them, and that can be gleaned as an order allowing for our present orientation.

In the late twentieth century, lacking a cosmological reference as an intersubjective ground for *praxis,* we cannot claim the luxury of merely being born into history like our predecessors before the nineteenth century. It is our task to interpret and appropriate these artifacts through our own prejudices and questions, always in reference to a collective project which, although it may remain uncertain (and may be forever unfinished) has clear cultural roots: a project beyond totality, clarity, and perspectivism which must be deployed in a relativistic space whose center is everywhere and whose circumference is nowhere. Such a project, ultimately related to knowledge as human orientation that is total and present, is one that we can only seek to construe through *poiësis,* the poetic act of making in our personal lives.

It is also important to recognize another related fallacy concerning context. Architectural meaning is *always* situational. In his wonderful book *Things: Four Metabletic Transformations,* J. H. van den Berg explains the primacy of perception in the constitution of human meaning and the articulation of what he calls primary and secondary structures.[2] Real common sense (as opposed to our omnipresent scientistic logical patterns of thought) shows, for example, that the perception of invariant colors or dimensions in the phenomena of our experience are secondary structures while the flow of experience itself is the given. Pure red or pure white are never empirical facts in our perceptual experience, and a vertical dimension is always perceived as larger than the horizontal dimension of the same quantitative extension. What we perceive as primary is always elastic time and distance, depending, for instance, on whether we go home from the office by bicycle or in a fast car, on whether we are hungry or bored.

If we think of St. Peter's Basilica in Rome, we may choose to objectify it as art historians often do, and state that its proportions are actually awkward and

Fig. 5.1. Piazza Pubblico, Vigevano, Italy: Bramante's arcade in the foreground, medieval tower in the background (1985). © Malcolm Quantrill

Fig. 5.2. Mantua, Italy: Street at the junction of the east end of the cathedral (1988). © Malcolm Quantrill

squat, except that Bernini's square makes it look right. Such intellectualizing ob-jectifications of architecture constitute a dangerous fallacy. St. Peter's Basilica is what it is in its existing site. The work never exists outside or apart from its con-text, even though we may wish to consider it as an autonomous geometrical ob-ject in the Cartesian space of our mind. Furthermore, the context is never purely the objectified site either. The context is part of the architecture and this latter is embodied differently in history, ranging from the archaic *daidala*[3] to ephemeral Renaissance and Baroque constructions for urban celebrations, or palaces like Versailles, whose architecture cannot be understood apart from its garden.

Thus we must conclude that context is, indeed, crucial for architectural mean-ing, particularly when understood in its more encompassing sense as situation or ground, or even as the "world of the work."[4] But while this may be true, it should also now be clear that the issue of the generation of appropriate architec-tural ideas in the modern world is a complex problem which cannot be resolved through a naive contextualism. Already at the time of Augustus, during the early Roman empire, Vitruvius spoke of "decorum" as one of the crucial aspects of ar-chitectural meaning, one that somehow was difficult to formulate in words and was thus set apart from the more easily objectifiable, mathematical categories of proportion, symmetry, and eurythmy.[5]

The modern world has a specific reality which is not independent from our thoughts. The world itself is an intentional phenomenon, and our world de-mands that our actions not become curtailed by a reactionary enslavement within prevailing traditions when these become empty of content. Heidegger—who has brought about the phenomenological awareness that lies at the root of my previ-ous remarks about the importance of the site as *locus* or place—writes: "The flight into tradition, out of a combination of humility and prescription, can bring about nothing in itself other than self-deception and blindness in relation to the historical moment."[6]

In this connection, we must also understand that architectural historians have created a delusion when they falsely try to explain the development of architec-ture as a progressive organic change. The great architecture which we now per-ceive as our tradition is in fact the work of enlightened individuals whose highly personal and imaginative syntheses were never "contextual" in the modern, nar-row sense of the word. These works were at the leading edge of culture and thought at the time they were created. They fit into the culture not because they were "underdesigned" or "formally coherent" but rather because their content—that which they represented, and which allowed their builders and inhabitants a deep sense of recognition—was the result of the individual architect's profound cultural grounding. This is precisely what is meant by architectural meaning: the symbolic role of architecture which, in its manifold historical embodiments, has allowed the individual inhabitant at different times in history and in all cultures, to belong to an institutional totality and transcend the mortal present.

Today the issue of cultural belonging cannot be taken for granted. In our times there seems to be a growing capacity of individuals to internalize culture. As a Mexican, for example, my most personal habits, gestures, and thoughts are grounded in my culture, but I also inhabit u-topia. The *locus* in the traditional sense has been disrupted, and this is a reality which must be acknowledged by architectural theory as *praxis.* Cultural values thus appear in architecture through the personal search which must be the task of the architect. They are embodied, but only (in)directly, through the body's deep recollection of Being. To expect that one can isolate cultural characteristics and reflect them in architecture through a conscious, externalized operation is naive. This kind of contextualism or regionalism has clearly failed to produce truly meaningful architecture that can be differentiated (except in a most superficial way) from building with similar intentions in other parts of the world.

82
Alberto
Perez-Gomez

This can hardly be surprising since even supposedly extreme ideological differences become meaningless when understood as superficial manifestations of a more fundamental, universal technological world-view.[7] To be sure, we have also inherited a very real capacity for reaction and personal reconciliation, the history of which, as an alternative poetic epistemology, starts with the inception of the Romantic movement.[8] Nonetheless this technological world-view, which originated in the seventeenth century and became a social reality in the early nineteenth century, is still the one in which we must deploy our actions. Today we live in an age when a new radicalized faith in applied science has become increasingly international and transcultural, fueled by ever more efficient systems of communication and information, blurring traditional boundaries and, with them, the qualities of specific places engaged in everyday modern life.

We also often witness an equally naive discussion about the notion of "urban public space" in post-industrial city. Much writing in this regard is merely wishful thinking. A parallelogram with four little trees does not make a *piazza,* and Postmodern simulations are not the modern equivalent of the *locus* where traditional architecture fulfilled its intersubjective, cultural promise to become a cosmic space, offering a ground and orientation to our finite lives. Richard Sennet has produced an excellent analysis of this problem.[9] The street and the square are not merely material, formal realities; they are also mental, part of culture. Regardless of how much we may admire the beautiful urban spaces of European cities, modern man does not participate in his culture through them. Whether Americans or Europeans, in Los Angeles or Rome, we are all voyeurs, mere tourists in these spaces. If we must accept that today we are condemned to this mode of togetherness, we must recognize that media such as television are more authentically "public." Urban "figures" may imply typicality, but if the typical figures are void of meaning, new forms of dwelling must be sought, even though

we must not forget that figural quality depends on recognition and that recognition was indeed the original purpose of the "symbol" (the token of friendship) in early Greek times, the objective of *mimesis*.[10]

Christian Norberg-Schulz, one of the most articulate defenders of a nostalgic brand of contextualism from a supposedly phenomenological perspective, has himself recognized that the loss of public interest is a crucial dilemma,[11] but he is not prepared to face the consequences squarely. Although in addressing the problem of modern urban space he puts forward a convincing critique of empty formalism, he chooses a poor example to make his point: the architecture of Aldo Rossi. This choice is paradoxical and revealing. It would be impossible to do justice here to Rossi's important and complex work, but it must be emphasized in connection to our concern that Rossi's projects are by far the most sensitive of those by architects who address directly the reality of the European city. The void in Rossi's architecture is a metaphysical enigma and it is totally intentional. His attitude to the "site" or the "context" approximates that of surrealist artists vis-à-vis the objects of our everyday life: a touching revelation of the mysterious at the core of the banal, an unveiling of that which the city might be, but is no longer. Furthermore, only after Rossi has drawn his poetic vision do we realize that what he has invented and disclosed is a "type." Not surprisingly (and with some notable exceptions), Rossi's most fascinating work must remain in the realm of the theoretical project.

Let me reiterate: The problems of the modern city, its alienation and anonymity, cannot be solved by assuming that the questions of dwelling, such as orientation and identification, are purely the result of formal configurations. A thorough understanding of history demonstrates that ritual, as the embodiment of myth, constituted the invisible referential order for the material, traditional orders in architecture to appear as meaningful at all scales, in the way we admire them in the old European cities.[12] The problem is that such ritual, understood as actions which truly revealed the place of man within a cosmological totality, is no longer a common source of existential orientation in modern everyday life. Of these rituals, only fragmented traces remain, in collective actions or in the conventionalized situations of dogmatic religions.

Norberg-Schulz and other apologists of Postmodernism have failed to recognize that the world and the body image finally ceased to be "classical" in the early nineteenth century. Neither the world nor the body is merely natural and constant. No one can argue with the recent popular preference for an architecture of concrete, qualitative places, rather than the construct of abstract space, an argument repeated often by those architects and planners who have realized the limitations of early modernism. But the problem of grounding our own architecture cannot be resolved through a simple-minded extrapolation from historical buildings. The theory of functionalism obviously failed, becoming prey to its own reductionist obsessions. It is unfair, nevertheless, to blame the problems of the city on our inability to produce a meaningful architecture. Regardless of what architects themselves may have said or written about their work, true modern architecture has been produced and is not identical to technological building. Some modern architecture has immense symbolic power, from Gaudí's Casa Mila to Aalto's Paimio Sanatorium or Villa Mairea, from Mies's Barcelona Pavilion to Le Corbusier's La Tourette or Ronchamp. Regardless of its "style," or of its more or less figural or abstract quality, such architecture allows for cultural recognition; it allows for *our* dreams, it represents *our* values without clarification, in a mode ultimately irreducible to discourse. On the other hand, the conventional buildings of the modern city do not generally reflect architectural intentions, but rather the clearly articulated dominant views of technology, ideology, or reactionary politics.

It is indeed important to emphasize that we have to be at home in our cities, to share a sense of existential, and not merely physical, security. Today, however, our collective home must accept a dimension of u-topia, one which accompanies the true values of modernity: the possibility of real (not scientist) historical evolution and our self-assertion as individuals, leaving behind the repugnant prejudices of the past and transcending both totalitarianism and anarchy. We must therefore embrace the positive aspects of u-topia, regardless of the historical debris that may or may not have accumulated in our particular city (depending, of course, on which part of the world we may live in and how ancient our original culture may be). Abstract architectural ideas evidently pose a danger of being easy to assimilate into the aims of technological domination. The power of the modern architect as an artist, however, should not be denied. The great works of modern architecture, even though they are in the world and belong to culture, like gestures or food, are comparatively free from the traditional limitations and associations of the specific site. Only by accepting that this is our reality and facing it straight on will we be able to transcend its dangers.

There is obviously no creation *ex nihilo*. A phenomenological understanding of meaning shows clearly that the world precedes us. In this sense the artist merely reveals the unnameable, which is what the symbol represents, the concealed deep reality of our human world. (The archaeologist of the future will always be able to date a work, no matter how "wild".) But this reality is only apparent in the intentional realm: we make it. The inveterate dualistic distinction between nature and culture is a fallacy. The structure of "ground, sky, and horizon" to which the poet and architect must allude is always present. However, without a purposeful invisible order (embodied in the past by the traditional religions that effectively operated at the level of society's everyday life), this cosmic structure is insufficient to generate a meaningful architecture. Place can no longer be simply disclosed, it has to be reinvented. Nature as the purposeful realm of God is no longer directly accessible and has been effectively superseded by simulations. A phenomenological exploration dealing with reality must acknowledge this problem, rather than elude it.

Fig. 5.4. Piazza Pubblico, Vigevano, Italy: Seventeenth-century Baroque church facade seen from beneath Bramante's arcade (1985). © Malcolm Quantrill

86
**Alberto
Perez-Gomez**

Suggesting that we can recognize purely material qualities—typological, topological, or morphological—at each one of the different scales addressed by the planner or architect, in order to build a figural architecture, in a supposedly identifiable "place" with its particular *genius loci,* is a delusion. If the intention is *dwelling* in the late twentieth century, the problem is rather to reinvent the ground of architecture by identifying first our renewed, non-Cartesian body image and its particular and necessarily fragmented recollection of Being. Through an introspective search, in the form of self-knowledge *through making,* the architect can generate order (by necessity geometrical, in the sense of a "taking measure" of the earth and its gravity), without giving up the quest for figuration. The recent theoretical projects of John Hejduk, particularly his Berlin masques, provide an excellent example of how this can be accomplished.

The archetypal ground of meaning is not directly accessible today from any set of prescriptions, regardless of how enlightened these may be. The age of architectural treatises modelled after Vitruvius or Alberti ended long ago, because the *mythos* which sustained scientific architectural theory as *logos* has been excluded from our culture and is no longer considered legitimate knowledge. The search is a personal one and, in this sense, is intimately related to the search of the painter, the writer, or the musician. The embodiment of the archetypal is today closer to the universal than to the specific (think of Rothko's chapel in Houston), and it must be capable of sustaining its meaning beyond particular sites. We must realize that the sites in a modern urban structure, if we merely "name" them like a Roman augur (or document them like a modern contextualist architect or planner), remain necessarily in a seventeenth-century perspective world: the quantitative, homogeneous space of perspective which is assumed to be the unshakable ground of our collective (scientific) truths (and the unspoken premise of architectural representations as projections or surrogates of buildings, from mere plans and elevations to computer-generated imagery), is the ultimate limitation of a site as "place."

As we have already implied, the only possible vehicle remaining for the generation of a truly seductive, vibrant architecture, one which we may inhabit with our contemporary imagery, memories, and dreams, is *personal making,* vis-à-vis a profound understanding of our world of genetic engineering and potential apocalypse. No matter how hard we try, we will not design and build in the contemporary city an archetypal tower, or cities that are "really" like Siena and possess culturally effective public spaces, or institutions that through a bit of formal cosmetics once again give us a foothold in the world. The solution is neither the Postmodernism of Michael Graves's Portland Public Services Building, Disneylands, and shopping malls nor, as Norberg-Schulz writes, "the forms of the past . . . back again as possible choices, in particular the classical ones, because the classical language represents the most universal and coherent figurative system so far known."[13] Two hundred years after Piranesi, Viel, Boullée and Ledoux recognized the end of Vitruvianism because the myths had vanished and classical architecture had become meaningless due to its lack of semantic ground, it is a sad comment on our architectural culture to come back to the recent, popular Postmodernist conclusions.[14]

Recent discussions on the role of language as the veritable house of Being, starting in the late works of Heidegger and continuing in the more recent texts on hermeneutics by Hans-Georg Gadamer and Paul Ricoeur, open up new possibilities for an understanding of the grounding of our making as architects. The role of poetic language to reveal the appropriateness of form appears most clearly in theoretical projects, of which the previously mentioned works by John Hejduk are a good example. What definitely does not follow from this discussion is the purported eternal value of classical architecture identified by Postmodernism as the poetic, figural language of architecture. Language may have an existential function, but it also changes historically. We must also remember that although language lies at the root of our humanity, it always alludes to an unarticulated ground which, although unnameable, rests even deeper in our embodied presence in the world. All that is worth saying is, indeed, translatable, even if the poetry must be rewritten. Thus, we may have access to Shakespeare's English, but his is not, nor should it be, our poetic language. Furthermore, the analogy with language can easily reinforce the illusion of a necessary material continuity, translated by many recent critics into "types" and "contextualism" when the discussion is focused on architecture. Such attempts are condemned to failure.

The alternative is to recognize that through poetic naming, the personal discovery of the architect/poet may find its archetypal roots, its program of poetic inhabitation. Seeking to translate for today and in terms of our own pressing questions the inveterate symbolic content embodied in the artifacts of our tradition, the modern architect may thus succeed in the task of touching, moving, and recollecting, opening for the spectator a gap to catch a furtive glimpse of Being in the vivid present of experience.

Notes

1. This refers to Peter Eisenman's "The End of the Classical," *Perspecta* 21, (1984). I take issue with the Deconstructivist foundation of architectural theory.

2. J. H. van den Berg, *Things: Four Metabletic Transformations* (Pittsburgh: Duquesne University Pres, 1970).

3. See my article "The Architect's Metier: An Exploration into the Myth of Dedalus," *Section A,* 2:5–6, (1985).

4. In the sense of contemporary hermeneutics, particularly in the work of Paul Ricoeur. See, for example, his *Hermeneutics and the Human Sciences* (Cambridge: Cambridge University Press, 1982).

5. Vitruvius M. P., *The Ten Books on Architecture* (New York: Dover, 1960), Book 1, ch. 2.

6. Martin Heidegger, "The Age of the World-Picture," *The Question Concerning Technology* (New York: Garland Publishing, 1977), 136.

7. In the sense of Jacques Ellul, *The Technological Society* (New York: Vintage, 1964).

8. Particularly in the German context with the works of the Schlegel brothers, Novalis, and Mme. de Stael. For an excellent discussion of the Romantic movement in relation to the issues of contemporary epistemology see G. Gusdorf, *Fondements du savoir romantique* (Paris: Payot, 1982).

9. See R. Sennet, *The Fall of Public Man* (Cambridge: Cambridge University Press, 1976).

10. See Hans-Georg Gadamer, *The Relevance of the Beautiful* (Cambridge: Cambridge University Press, 1986) and also Christian Norberg-Schulz, *The Concept of Dwelling* (New York: Rizzoli, 1985), 66.

11. Christian Norberg-Schulz, *Concept of Dwelling,* 69.

12. Ibid.

13. Norberg-Schulz, *Concept of Dwelling,* 133–34.

14. In this regard, see my own *Architecture and the Crisis of Modern Sciences* (Cambridge, Mass.: MIT Press, 1983).

Off Limits: City Pattern and City Texture
Joseph Rykwert

6

Although their buildings, if you take them one by one, were at best insignificant and often dreary, the English new towns, which were planned to diffuse some of the metropolitan crises and also prevent (as they successfully did for a while) the uncontrollable spread of suburbia, have been very successful in providing an urban environment for a large population, their planners also experimented successfully in providing some of the first pedestrian precincts in Europe.

While Stevenage and the other new towns were going up in Britain two American scholars, Morton and Lucia White, were gathering material for a book which was to appear in 1962.[1] Their book, *The Intellectual versus the City,* shows how American men of letters, from Thomas Jefferson to Frank Lloyd Wright, were consistently and articulately hostile to the city as an institutional fabric. The Whites consider at length Henry James's attitude to the city in which he had done much of his work, and they quote a meditation on London in which Hyacinth Robinson, the male lead in James's *Princess Casamassima,* damns its "great ulcers and sores—the sick eternal misery crying out of the darkness in vain, confronted with granaries and treasure houses and places of delight where shameless satiety kept guard." Like his hero, James both loved and hated London.

Of course, the note of hostility to all things urban could be found in British writers equally powerfully; what is more, Latin satirists could supply an abundance of hostile and spiteful attitudes. However, since the Whites published their book, there has been a noticeable change of opinion among writers in English; the anti-urban intellectual now seems a figure from the past. What is true of writers is almost equally true of architects, whom I must count, some evidence to the contrary notwithstanding, among the intellectuals. Again, this may well be due to economic pressure: the intellectual, as a money-earning member of society, has moved from public service and the journals to the academy; this is due in part to the increasing bureaucratization of western society, and partly to the enormous expansion of the universities. Because—Oxbridge notwithstanding—the British university is tied into an urban situation, and the intellectual cannot afford to be violently at odds with his immediate environment, the hostility of which the Whites wrote has inevitably been modified in Britain at least. And yet that same hostility, which operated on intellectual life when the cities of the world were growing at an unprecedented rate, has had an effect which, I think, has been quite overwhelming.

To go back to Henry James—with London he had a love-hate affair. But New York he loathed for being "a pin-cushion in profile." It was not quite yet the pin-cushion we now know, the silhouette which has become a model for most world cities; it was developed when most of the writers whom the Whites anthologized were writing. This profile is in fact the product of market forces pushing up through the net of the grid pattern.

The grid plan is an intermittently fascinating phenomenon, and it is regarded by most historians and theorists of architecture or planning as a neutral device which can be used to produce almost any kind of effect. Anything can grow out of or be puréed by the grid. In the case of New York, it has become a set of Cartesian coordinates on which the graph of land prices can be drawn. As you approach Manhattan from the Long Island airports—or indeed if you approach it in any other way—you see a transposed graph of land values, and that is what the city *represents*. In that sense it is useful to think of New York (or any other similar city) not as a work of art, but as a piece of nature in the raw; it is the untilled and ungarnished product of natural, or rather quasi-natural, forces—in the sense that some of us would maintain that market forces have a movement and power over which no control can be exercised.

Writers on architecture and the city have been fond of comparing the pincushion effect of American cities (and have justified it by this comparison) with a very different silhouette which will be familiar to many of my audience: the town of San Gimigniano in Tuscany. It is very small, and numbered about three thousand inhabitants at the end of the last century. Its pincushion silhouette of towers has both a different cause—the armed rivalry between the main landholding families of the neighborhood—and a quite different effect from that of the New York skyscrapers. The tallest tower in the town is not that of any family, but that of the Palazzo del Popolo, the town hall: at 174 feet, it is by far the tallest building in the town. The next tallest, the bell tower at 167 feet, set the height up to which the private towers may reach: no family tower may go higher than that.

Such a rule applied in many other towns. In Milan, until quite recently, the eighteenth-century gilt Madonna—*Madonnina*—on the cathedral lantern was the same point of reference. In Philadelphia, it was the statue of William Penn which stands on the tower of City Hall. Both of these conventions have recently been broken, but the San Gimigniano rule was never breached. In bigger Italian towns —Bologna, Florence, Perugia, Siena—you will find similar towers, similar rules, as you would also find them in Hanseatic towns. Showily excessive building height was always reproved, and controlled by the dominant height of public building; and public building always had annexed to it, as did the diminutive town hall in San Gimigniano, a paved, accessible public space, which was both meeting place and institutional center, where the city could "represent" itself to its citizens and be a presence in their daily business.

Our cities are inevitably different. Institutions and monuments appear shrunken and reduced; our cities are dominated by two quite different kinds of built fabric. One is the strident crowd of office buildings, the pincushion; the other—and its complement—is the lackluster carpet of housing. In the maze fabricated by sanitary and traffic engineers, the citizen can have no sense that his house is enhanced by its orientation or its placing inside a pattern which might give him a sense of his role in the work and the institutional life of the city. The house, we know, is not a home.

This perhaps too simple picture has been complicated by the insistence of local governments that the lower income groups should be accommodated in high-rise buildings of all sorts; but the suburban carpet remains the Anglo-Saxon's preferred housing mode. The two patterns are interdependent, so that even early in the 1920s a rental building such as the Woolworth Tower in lower Manhattan required vast areas of footpath and roadway for its users and for the parking of vehicles, while in 1924 Sir Raymond Unwin had already foreseen the stress of the high-rise block on the pattern of the grid.[2] Of course this pressure has grown out of all proportion with the enormous increase in car ownership. The correlative is the usual undifferentiated suburban layout, most commonly the product of road surface laid over a drainage plan, in which the building plots are the negative of the road pattern. The result of this dichotomy has been that we do not think of the city as having any shape at all. "Housing" has become a neutral and undiscriminating activity which makes demands neither of the private home nor on the corporate—let alone the public—office. This reduction also leaves the grid plan as the inert and mechanical instrument of the utilitarian planner.

The ultimate mechanical grid may well be the "ideal" plan which Ludwig Hilberseimer worked out in Chicago.[3] The huge H-shaped blocks are grouped in couples off motorways, and the grid lines cross at cloverleaf junctions: it is the almost perfect statement of grid roadway and mass housing. There is of course no room in such a plan for any interpretation: this is the grid as the self-evident project, a geometrical entity, the obvious product of rational land division.

Hilberseimer's plan was done when building skills were at a low ebb, from which they have never quite recovered. The deliberate reduction of the building process to mechanical operation was accomplished with the enthusiastic collaboration, almost under the leadership, of the most prominent architects—not that they had much choice in the matter. However, the buildings in Hilberseimer's plan are clearly built very much like those of his friend and collaborator Mies van der Rohe, whose adherence to the new fabrication was almost theological.

There are other ways of coping with this situation. Mies's exalted attitude failed to reckon with the speed with which the simplifications of building form promoted by industrialization would play into the hands of unscrupulous developers and equally unscrupulous (though differently motivated) politicians. It is all a matter of recent history and lengthy laments; yet earlier in the century there were attempts to exercise a measure of choice and assertion of value, even within the operation of the grid plan. The Radburn Plan, which had been developed out of Clarence Perry's neighborhood idea for a New Jersey suburb of New York in 1928,[4] was adopted as a basis for the layout of housing in several English new towns, and although favored for its ingenious way with traffic as well as for its social amenity, it also required the assertive presence of public and institutional buildings. It therefore presupposed an interpretation and inflection, however modest, of the grid plan, such as was not attempted, for instance, in the twisting of the grid at Milton Keynes.[5] Even a nursery school can take on that function, since around it a public space is inevitably created. This was not regarded with much interest by new-town planners, although it is what distinguishes the Radburn-derived layout from the normal developers' suburban plan. And indeed the city of high-rise blocks and skyscrapers does not have any public space of that kind.

What has happened since has not yet had its historian, though it badly needs one. The increasing bureaucratization of our society harnessed the simplified building process to implant huge building complexes for new international organizations in crucial points of old cities: the United Nations in Rome, UNESCO in Paris, the European Community and Parliament in Brussels and Strasbourg; and they have all displayed our monumental impotence. All of them, like monstrous cuckoos, have fouled the cities in which they have nested. This is partly due to the wretched architectural quality of the buildings themselves, but also to the inability of the planners and architects to relate these buildings to the existing urban pattern at all, or to demonstrate by the fabric the importance and vast power of the bodies which they house.

Which returns me to the matter I left half-finished: the interpretation of the grid plan. What makes it rather difficult to interpret is the contempt which many of my contemporaries reserve for the intellectual achievements of our ancestors. The treatment of the grid plan is an instance of just that; this ingenious device, which should be seen as the result of a concentrated and admirable effort, is treated as the all-too-obvious by-product of rational land division, therefore as obvious— and therefore of no real interest. We all know, further, that the Romans were particularly partial to the grid plan. Figure 6.1 shows a plan of the tract of land

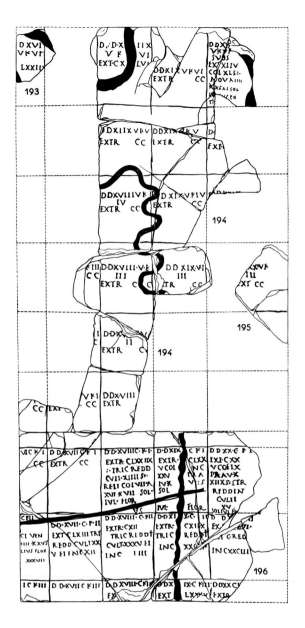

Fig. 6.1. Land division between Pierrelatte and Donzère recorded on the marble plan of Orange, Section B, slab III J, ca. A.D. 75. Orange, Musée Archéologique. After A. Piganiol, *Les Documents Cadastraux de la Colonie Romaine d'Orange.* Paris 1962.

Fig. 6.2. Fragments 193–95 of the marble map of Orange, section B, slab III J. After A. Piganiol.

which includes the towns of Avignon, Orange, and Montélimar, which Roman surveyors had laid out for land division among new settlers and colonists. The distance from Orange (*Arausia*) to Grignan is about twenty miles, and that provides a useful scale for comparison, since Manhattan Island is about sixteen miles at its longest. The layout is known both from aerial surveys and from fragments of a large marble map which recorded the land titles in the district and which was displayed in the Forum of Orange (see fig. 6.2).

Inevitably, therefore, if you read the accounts of Roman towns in the handbooks and the usual histories, they will tell you that towns in this country whose names end in "-chester" are laid over Roman military camps (*castra*), and that Roman towns are grid-planned, since the Romans were a highly efficient, organized, and militaristic people who made their towns in the same way as they made their barracks. This seems to me not only beside the point but actually very misleading about Roman ways and Roman intentions—and therefore about the nature of our heritage.

If you look at the surviving textbooks of the Roman surveyors, you will find the rather surprising and Christian-looking picture of the cross in a blue star-studded circle as the foundation image of the discipline, which its authors claim had divine founders and was in some way like the discipline of sky-diviners (*augurs*).[6] But it is an antique and pagan image. The cross within a circle was the sign of the *templum,* the augurs' diagram, which had to be drawn on the ground with a special curved staff, and "projected" onto a landscape before the omens—lightning, falling stars, bird flight, or other animals—were observed. To read such omens and to act accordingly was the business of every Roman magistrate, and the word "inaugurate" has passed from this custom into our common speech. The gods would not always oblige, but could be helped in various ways to make their intentions clear. There were many skeptics, of course, and soothsayers' mistakes were gleefully recorded. Nevertheless, these rites were practiced daily, and all Roman buildings which were so "inaugurated" were called *templa,* although they were not necessarily temples in our sense. Near the door they would be signed with a cross of the kind shown in figure 6.3, inscribed with two words from the augurs' formulae: *postica, antica*—"hither" and "thither" which, together with "left" and "right," quartered the augur's horizon as the *cardo* and the *decumanus* quartered the Roman military camp and the city.

Fig. 6.3. Bronze cross fixed to a stone block, probably a doorjamb, of the temple of Aesculapius at Lambesis in North Africa. After P. Monceaux, "Note sur une Croix de Bronze trouvée à Lambèse" (C.-R. Ac.Inscr. & B. L. 1920).

Roman surveying was technically simple: a bronze cross was held on a pivot, the end of each arm having a plumb line attached to it; a fifth plumb line hung from the center, and that was suspended over a stone, on which the crossing of the two main lines of the augural and surveying diagram was usually inscribed. The surveyor worked by aligning the sightings of two or more such instruments. The augurs' and the surveyors' methods were closely interconnected: both were world diagrams, representations of world order.

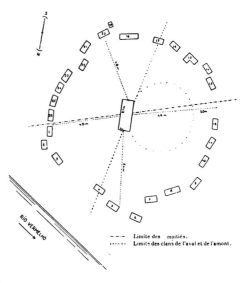

If you were a Roman military commander, you could not set up camp for the night without performing such ceremonies; as a surveyor, you moved to stigmatize unknown, "wild" land, to take possession of it by branding it with the mark of world order. The grid plan is the direct development of the *templum.* In a Roman town it was commemorated at every street corner in the stones which marked the location in blocks from the original crossing lines, from the stone on which the surveyor had made his first sighting.

But the process has a more archaic and perhaps an even more important background, one from which a great deal can be learned about the way our forefathers ran their collective life. At very low levels of material culture, in villages of improvised huts of twigs and dry grass, the flimsy buildings concealed a complex and demanding organization of terrain. In the case of the Bororo of the western Amazon basin (see fig. 6.4), whose doings were recorded by Claude Lévi-Strauss in the 1940s,[7] we know not only about the contrast between the wretched building and the rich elaboration of ceremonial attire, but we know too that the rough circle of the village was divided into moieties (see fig. 6.5), and that within each moiety there was a triple organization of huts which governed such important matters as the degrees of kinship and the choice of spouse (see fig. 6.6). The elaborate conceptual apparatus which governed village life was present to every inhabitant. What seems to us merely a rough group of smaller huts huddling round one larger one, the men's house, was to the inhabitants a complicated,

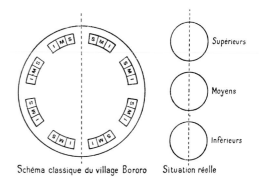

Fig. 6.7. Funeral dance in Kejara village. After C. Lévi-Strauss.

detailed diagram which the villagers carried in their heads and which governed their relationships and also showed the meaning of the passage of the seasons (see fig. 6.7).

Such ideas persist and survive in strange ways. The diagram of the cross in the circle is one of the most pervasive and elaborately varied ornaments of early pottery from Neolithic and Chalcolithic cultures. Inevitably, pots thrown on a wheel are circular, yet the cross-in-circle diagram is not their obvious ornament. However its implication seems to me fairly clear. All pots are potential divination pots. As all meat eaten in primitive society was the result of either a hunt or a sacrifice, so all pots were potential divination vessels. Even now, were you to visit fortune-tellers who use (as they often do) tea leaves or coffee grounds, you would find that they are relying on the same world-order diagram as the one used by the Roman augur. The same system is still used elsewhere in other ways: by African diviners from a throw of beans, by geomancers of all kinds.[8] The grid plan derived its force and its attraction from this root notion, the crossing of two lines at right angles in a circle, from which the grid is derived by extension.

To help me explain what I mean, let me introduce a distinction here. Like the Romans, the Greeks founded many colonies; they also consulted omens and oracles in the course of foundation rites, and they planned them on orthogonal lines.

The current problem of our cities is rather different. I started by making reference to the not altogether acceptable face of the new towns, in the Stevenage town center. Let me remind you of another aspect, thought by some to be even less acceptable: Cumbernauld town center, one of the two real megastructures built in Britain during the 1960s (the other is in Bloombury; the Parkhill development in Sheffield, though much bigger, remained a complex of slab blocks). The Cumbernauld complex is a huge city center for a relatively small town, yet it fails to be representative of institutions. Isolated from the carpet layout of most of the housing, it emulates the relation between pincushion and carpet suburb.

It is worth insisting on this point, I think, because the power of Sixtus V's planning lay precisely in his clear vision of how institutional related to formal, how representative and public related to private and infill. The physical structure of the city of Rome remained a clear image, representing to the citizen the institutional structure of the public life in which he moved. I have rushed you from ancient Greeks and Romans to L'Enfant. I can demonstrate nothing in such a rush; but I can suggest, however tentatively, that the pattern of a successful urban plan must always be representational; and until we have also learned to deal with public life in architecture, and have returned an image of public life and dignity to our institutions, we will not be able to project for a truly habitable city.

The recent decline of architecture cannot be corrected by adding fancy pieces to the business enterprise of housing people and corporations. At the beginning of this essay, I mentioned complaints about "soulless" building. Much of the criticism of modernity which goes by the label Postmodern has been concerned with the addition of ornament to machine-made building, as if the soul of the building lay entirely on its surface. But this shallow resolution of our problems has in fact been tried, at least once before—at the beginning of the 1960s—and it failed then. That is why resolution of city center into object-buildings, designer skyscrapers, seems to me as faulty as reliance on the multipurpose megastructure to resolve the problems of urban living. Yet we must recognize that planning, or urbanism as some now prefer to call it, is wholly dependent on architecture; that planning can never be two-dimensional and can never allow the third dimension of height to look after itself; zoning and plot ratios will never provide the answers we require.

Adding fancy bits of agreeable historical and nostalgic allure to the tried and unloved pieces of urban texture will not answer either. The reality with which our buildings have to deal, which they have to interpret, is that of the smooth spaghetti junction and the scale of urban transit. You may find me frivolous, discussing such matters while our cities are under siege. But designer skyscrapers are on the advance. London, a city in which the pattern has never been quite strong enough, is about to be assaulted by an overgrowth of a part of its texture. Such developments must parasitize the pattern, leaving it weaker and poorer. I

Fig. 7.1. Aldo Andreani —Palazzo Fidia, side on Via Serbelloni, Milan. Main Entry.

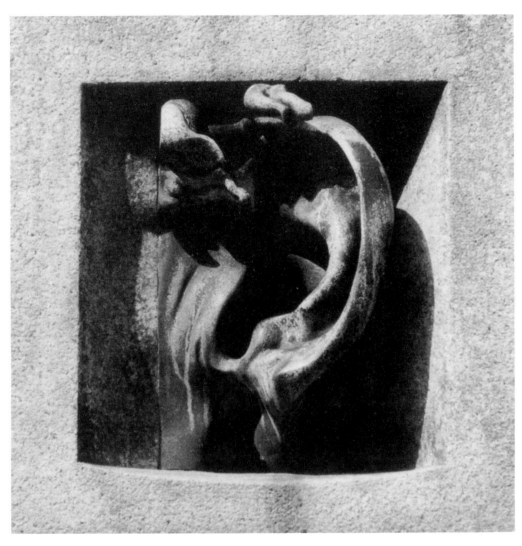

Fig. 7.2. Aldo Andreani —Palazzo in Via Serbelloni, Milan. Detail of intercom for porter's lodge.

out of position and being offended by something or someone who upsets with grotesque images the serene canons and moral anodyne of the bourgeois esthetic sense. In 1928, near Palazzo Fidia in Via Serbelloni, a side street off Via Mozart in the same subdivision as Terra Sole Busca, Andreani designed another palazzo, another luxury apartment building. There the clue to the meaning of the embodiment theory may be found in a piece of sculpture, a bronze ear inserted in the wall, a disguised intercom marking the porter's lodge (fig. 7.2). This easy mockery is redeemed by the masterly execution which becomes the physical expression of a magic charm to achieve an effect in a symbolic manner.[14] The ear in the wall is the left ear since Gargantua was born through that ear. Rabelais recounts the epic of Gargantua's birth: Gargamelle, Gargantua's mother, was suffering from a prolapsed uterus and also from having eaten but not digested too much carnival tripe at the moment of the delivery. Her condition made access to

Fig. 7.7. Aldo Andreani
—Palazzi Comunali,
Mantua. Section show-
ing the joint between
vetus and *novus* for
Piazza Broletto.

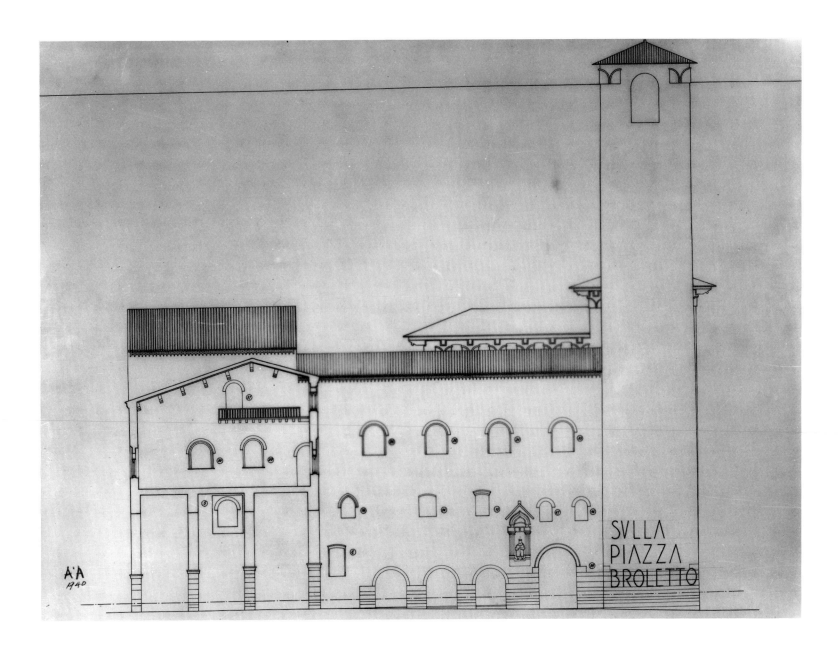

Fig. 7.8. Aldo Andreani
—Palazzi Comunali,
Mantua. Elevation of
Piazza Broletto.

If seen through the magnifying glass of the architectural historians, who pigeon-hole and adorn their findings with the cobweb-like traces of the relationships existing between different schools or groups of design, this Mantuan architect belongs to the grimy group of the minors. Able at upsetting the passer-by, by presenting something never seen before or perhaps seen too many times in diverse buildings, something not digested or too well-digested and therefore transformed, Andreani's *a latere* position has never been recognized on the official pages of architectural history. An architect gifted with a creative imagination but who has not produced a school, and who has not created for contemporary critics and colleagues the same sense of wonder which halted scandalized passers-by at the foot of Palazzo Fidia—such an architect belongs to footnotes. The inhabitants of a city are more sensible of the human facts embodied in the built forms than are the critics of architecture, who are more curious about styles than about stimuli.

To understand Andreani's work we should not place his buildings within the framework of history, but rather develop a story in which human bodies trip over stones which then became the causes of scandal. This story is a "gay" story in the sense that "gay" is the science devised by Nietzsche; and stones play a major role in Nietzsche's cry:

> The stone is more stone than before. In general we no longer understand architecture, at least by far not in the same way we understand music. We have outgrown the symbolism of lines and figures, as we have grown unaccustomed to the tonal effects of rhetoric, no longer having sucked in this kind of cultural mother's milk from the first moment of life. Originally everything about a Greek or Christian building meant something, and in reference to a higher order of things. The atmosphere of inexhaustible meaningfulness hung about buildings like a magic veil. Beauty entered in the system only secondarily, impairing the basic feeling of uncanny sublimity, of sanction by magic or the Gods' nearness. At the most beauty tempered the dread—but this dread was the prerequisite everywhere.[24]

Andreani's buildings are dreadful. From the Philistine point of view of the historian, a building like Andreani's Mantuan Camera di Commercio (Chamber of Commerce) of 1910–11, an aggregate of too many styles, is a visual calamity; whereas for the inhabitants and for the habitual passer-by the edifice is a grotesque narrative in which stones are no longer stones, but bodies, poles of tactile attraction, a concentrate of imagination, stating provocatively the progression of the past (fig. 7.9). It is an architecture that gives you "habits," the true dimension of buildings, not the tourist's visual perception but the tactile character of a habitual dwelling.

A terrific but not terrifying building is that Mantuan Camera di Commercio. Local architectural criticism saw in it a celebration of the forms of the tradition of the Mantuan quattrocento. Only a few traces of this local stylistic tradition are

Fig. 7.9. Aldo Andreani
—Loggia Dei Mer-
canti, Camera di Com-
mercio, Mantua. Ele-
vation drawing.

detectable in the building—one of the first buildings designed by Andreani—which is perhaps burdened with too many other historical and stylistic references. The architectural citations used by Andreani are perspicuous, but what makes this building unique in the Neomedievalist movement is the idea of project.

An architectural *project* is a continuous sign and results from an uninterrupted act of design based on a continuous search for the human measure that bridges the past and future of the constructed world. An architectural project is not the designing of a specific building, but is rather a projection of a future constructed world based on the transformation of the past world of construction through a specific design.[25] This idea of architectural project is the norm in grotesque architecture. In Mantua, the projects were there before Andreani's work was done. What Andreani does as a responsive architect is not only to recognize what has not yet been designed, but also to probe its nature in such a way that the edifice seems preexisting in the latent conditions of the site. This is most clearly evident in Andreani's restoration. He perceived the historical monuments of a city to be a stratification of incomplete projects. In these projects the in-complete is present in the complete, as in his architectural drawings the in-visible is in the visible. Andreani's architecture is *in* the world of the *visible*. This means that the bodies of architecture surround our bodies. Architecture and the human body face one another and between the two there is "not a frontier, but a contact surface"[26] which determines our perceptions of the habitual. In Andreani's work that which conforms to our habits has always been there before, because of the altered chronological order of the grotesque project. Buildings which came later, inserted in the city which was earlier, become a "before," as the Schirolli House is before the Rio, the city canal, onto which it is inserted. The same is true for the Nuvolari House, which is before the architectural "after" of Via Chiassi, the street it faces.

The deformation of chronological logic is also manifested in the use of materials such as the stone selected for both Casa Nuvolari and the Camera di Commercio, a tabular sandstone called *ceppo di gre*. The hardness, cavities, and color of this stone can make the construction appear on the one hand as if it has been consumed by the passing of time, or on the other hand as if the building has not yet been made sound by the passing of time. In other words, the building can look too young or too old. But what is the line that separates what is decaying and what is in formation? The base of the Camera di Commercio is so vague! It looks as if it had been worn away by the passing of time and weather, but at the same time it appears as if the construction has never been completed. Furthermore, the *ceppo di gre* is a natural stone that looks like an artificial conglomerate. To force the chronological logic of things also means to discuss the limits between natural and artificial, as Andreani does in many buildings where the necessity of artifice is achieved naturally.

If we analyze Andreani's brief description of the project (*Relazione di progetto*) for the Camera di Commercio, we notice that the language is peculiar. The arcade is described as "grandiose" and of "large lines," but at the same time is "limited on two of the sides" and "narrow on the other two." The "high arches" are "sprightly," but at the same time "grave"; the whole palace has a "cool tone" but is simultaneously "hot in color."[27] The dominant figure in Andreani's writing is the oxymoron, a rhetorical trope which unites two contradictory terms that can be fruitfully interpreted together, so that one can generate a powerful criticism through an "eloquent silence" or reach an "obscure clarity" in design.[28] It is significant to recall that "esthetics" as a discipline began with an oxymoron. Alexander Baumgarten, who originated that field of study in the 1730s, explained that esthetics is a science dealing with "clearly confused representations." By this statement, he subverted the traditional sequential continuity existing between the categories of obscure and confused, clear and distinct conceptions by attributing perfection (*perfectio*) only to clearly confused conception.[29]

The oxymoron for Andreani is a sort of clearly confused idea which ought not to be seen as a step inside the design process, but as the process itself, a beautiful conceiving (*pulchre cogitandi*).[30] We should think of the Camera di Commercio as a black box where the material constituting the skin is nothing but an anticipation of the confused conglomeration of the interior. Analyzing Andreani's ability to combine building elements and materials, the edifice reveals a very clear confusion, a confusion aiming toward its own reproduction. The building plainly shows that Andreani designs the idea of construction rather than a finite building. Clearly confused representations are like "shining stones"[31] which cannot be broken into discrete pieces by means of analytic procedures, but they possess the power of self-reproduction: confused representations generate additional confused representations, *ad infinitum*.

In Andreani's work, the dominant oxymoron consists of the "skeleton" which is "antique" and the "physiognomy" (*sagoma*) which is "modern." How is it possible to unify in one project an old skeleton with a new physiognomy? The answer is the use of the grotesque figure, which is old and new at the same time: one sort of architectural oxymoron. This is something that Andreani learned during his investigations of the architecture of the Palazzi Comunali where it is impossible to distinguish the *vetus* and the *novus*. In this group of buildings, the before and the after are indistinguishable in the many modifications and transformations the edifices underwent during their long life as the seat of city government.

Andreani has no doubts about the hermeneutic value of historical-chronological ambiguities: the antique-modern oxymoron is the dominant imaginative technique he used to generate the grotesque anthropomorphism of his early buildings. It is an anthropomorphism without metaphors, since what is shown is not the look or the appearance of a building element, but rather the process by which such looks are generated by the hand or by the body of the designer. In Andreani's architecture the building elements carry on and are carried on by an amalgam of metonymies and metaphors, but their aggregation, their grafting together generates an architectural project, a metonymic expression which produces unique and finite images, their simultaneity negating the ineluctability of the arrow of time.

A project always has a chronological dimension for which a *before* and an *after* exist, a beginning point and an arrival point, in such a way that the process is hardly apparent. The process is implicit in the complete work; it is in-visible. Andreani makes the process completely visible, omitting whatever makes the object discreet. Stone after stone, the process is materialized in the early production of buildings, making clear the dynamic nature of formation refusing completion, and expressing the poetic depths of deformation, built up stroke after stroke like an architectural *chiaroscuro*.

An instance of this is the deformation of the capitals in the Loggia dei Mercanti (Merchants' Arcade) on the northeast side of the Camera di Commercio (fig. 7.10). After a sequence of metamorphoses, the last capital on the north side of the loggia grotesquely proposes the clearly confused beginning and end of a traditional interpretation of that building detail. In classical anthropomorphism, the canonical interpretation of the capital is an identification with the human head, but in the sequence of the capitals designed by Andreani the transformation is metonymic rather than metaphoric. The metaphor of the head is transformed into the metonymy of the helmet; the figurative source is the Greek helmet with the long frontal piece of protection for the nose, which seen in a ground-figure relationship recalls a phallic image. The last capital—or perhaps the first—is the evident icon of this metonymic manipulation, the representation in stone of a grotesque and sarcastic Italian idiom (*testa di cazzo*), a language carnival-like but fundamental for human communication.[32]

The same oxymoronic logic dominates in both groups of Milanese and Mantuan buildings. The buttress on the corner of Via Mozart and Via Melegari in Palazzo Fidia is a perfect instance, in which the flat nature of bricks is used to generate surfaces swollen with humors. This plush image is diagonally conjugated with hard and sharp images. Based on the canny use of the oxymoron are the "infinite modifications"[33] in which both the parts and the wholes of Andreani's buildings are involved. Infinite are the modifications which a brick can undergo in relation to a surface or to a given orthogonal axis. Infinite are the positions and the formal reverberations caused by the rotation of a brick. For instance the bricks marking the string course of Villa Zanoletti are rotated seven degrees more than in the string course of the Camera di Commercio, generating a different play of shadows. The effect is rustic and bucolic in the case of Villa Zanoletti, whereas the rotation of the bricks in the Camera di Commercio generates tense, dignify-

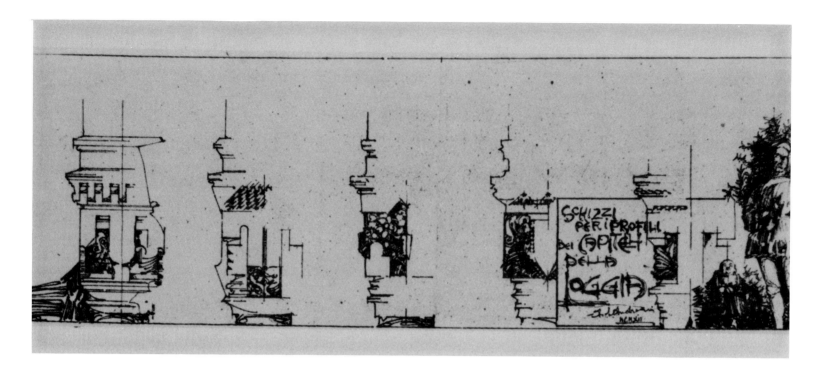

ing, and mercurial shadows proper to a place of the urban trade in products of the fertile ground of Lombardy.

Merely rotating a constructive object, such a brick, makes possible the production of different architectural figures. The figure of a constructive object is ephemeral until the modification in its status shows what it is not. Using 24 × 11 × 5.5-cm bricks, the logical way of building a vertical support is to relate the bricks on the shortest side. The result is a pilaster rather than a column. The shape of a column is based on a rotational geometry; it is a cylinder, not a prism. Andreani makes a column by rotating the bricks, as he does in the garden of the Villa Risi[34] where the bricks and the cylinder keep their nature, modifying themselves without annulling each other (figs. 7.11, 7.12). The same effect—modification without a change in status—is in the joint between the capital and the column in the entry hall of the same villa. The cylinder without entasis of the column penetrates the stone of an unsculpted capital, which assumes the nature of the artificial stone: the brick. The result is unexpectedly the stressing and celebrating of a joint between the materials that generally goes unnoticed. This ironic celebration of joints is based on a discreet use of the oxymoron in joining parts of different materials as in the Camera di Commercio, and on a sarcastic celebration of the joints between the sections of the same material as in the windows of Casa Nuvolari (fig. 7.13).

Fig. 7.10. Aldo Andreani—Loggia Dei Mercanti, Camera di Commercio, Mantua. Drawings of the capitals of the Loggia.

123

Fig. 7.11. Aldo Andre-
ani—Villa Risi, Andes
near Mantua.

Fig. 7.12. Aldo Andre-
ani—Villa Risi, Andes
near Mantua. Detail of
the entry columns.

Fig. 7.13. Aldo Andre-
ani — Nuvolari House,
Via Chiassi, Mantua.
Windows of the
building.

126
Frascari
and Sgarbi

I PALAZZI COMVNALI DI MANTOVA I BROLETTI, LA CHIESA NEL PERIODO AVREO

Fig. 7.14. Aldo Andreani—Hypothetical reconstruction of the Palazzi Comunali di Mantua during the Golden Age (Periodo Aureo).

When the invisible is in the visible, it is necessary to discuss the idea of beginning, which should not be confused with the idea of origin. Origin is God-given, whereas beginning is human. This oneiric tale of the architecture of Andreani demonstrates a paradigm in which "beginnings inaugurate deliberately another production of meaning,"[35] a production based on a grotesque body where deformation is the rule for generating meaning. The ontology of construction is in "de-formation"[36] since it is known that any building element is deformed by the load applied to it. This is the beginning of grotesque architecture, and it is the sudden measure of the architecture of Andreani. A traditional process of construction is used to remove what is well-known and to set the building on a continuous process of transformation whose arrival point is unknown. That point of arrival is always a point of beginning.

March 22, 1989[37]

Notes

1. For a discussion of theory as an exotic behavior see Hans Blumenberg, *Das Lachen der Thrakerin: Eine Urgeschichte der Theorie* (Frankfurt-am-Main: Suhrkamp, 1987), ch. 1.

2. Friedrich C. Nietzsche, *The Gay Science* (New York: Harper & Row 1974), aphorism 280.

3. As Gregotti points out in his editorial in the special issue of *Rassegna* (10:33, March 1, 1988) devoted to the work of Andreani, the work of that Mantuan architect followed a progression parallel to that of the modern movement. The first publication on Andreani's work was by Enrico Somaré—*Aldo Andreani architetto scultore* (Milano: Pizzi & Pizio, 1937)—who defined Andreani as "an artist of contrast." For a complete bibliographical survey of writings on Andreani see note 1 in Rossana Bosaglia, "Aldo Andreani artista contrastato," and note 1 in Amedeo Belluzzi, "La Camera di Commercio di Mantova e gli esordi architettonici," both in *Rassegna* (10:33), 6–11 and 12–32. In the same issue see also the "Regesto delle opere e progetti, 1909/1945."

4. The Precious Blood of Christ is preserved in a crypt under Alberti's Church of Sant' Andrea, designed by Anton Maria Viarni.

5. Giulio Pippi [Romano], *I Modi,* ed. Lynne Lawner (Milan: Longanesi, 1984).

6. In designing the profile of a pavilion, the designers imitated the contours of the body of the German dancer and of a large veil, and van de Velde wrote, "The art of Loïe Fuller holds the most beautiful thoughts of our time and the most beautiful material of the world. The rhythm, a divine instrument, consecrates the fusion, and we participate in the celebration of all we love in the way we love it—light, gold, life—life in the light and life in the shadow." Quoted by Giovanna Massorbio and Paolo Portoghesi, *Album del Liberty* (Bari: Laterza, 1975), 48–49. See also *Henri Sauvage 1873–1932* (Bruxelles: Archives d'Architecture Moderne, 1976). Sculptures of the dancer had been shown at the Turin Exhibition in 1902; see V. Pica, *L'arte decorativa all'esposizione di Torino del 1902* (Bergamo: Istituto italiano d'arti grafiche, 1903),

7. Quoted by Francesco Tentori, *Vita e opere di Le Corbusier* (Bari: Laterza, 1979), 82. To fully understand the presence of corporeality in the work of Le Corbusier it is sufficient to look to his drawings of women, which reveal how those forms had been incorporated in his designs.

8. Boccioni Futurista [Antonio Boccioni], *Pittura scultura Futuriste* (Milano: Edizioni Futuriste di Poesia, 1914), 173.

9. Vittorio Gregotti and Guido Cannella, "Il Novecento e l'architettura," *Edilizia Moderna* 81, (1963): 83–90.

10. Boccioni, *Pittura,* 225.

11. Cesare De Seta, *L'architettura del Novecento* (Turin: UTET, 1981), 47.

12. Vittorio Gregotti, "Milano e la cultura architettonica tra le due guerre," *Razionalismo e l'architettura Italiana durante il Fascismo* (Venice: La Biennale, 1976), 18.

13. Dino Buzzati, "Che strano altro ieri," *Corriere della Sera,* Jan. 5, 1971, quoted by Amedeo Belluzzi, "L'Architettura di Aldo Andreani," *Civiltà Mantovana,* 11 (1977): 307.

14. For a discussion of the role of magic in the production of art see Francesco Pellizzi, "Adventure of the Symbol: Magic for the Sake of Art," *Lectures on Constructed Thought* (New York: The Cooper Union, 1986), Lecture 1.

15. George Hersey, *The Lost Meaning of Classical Architecture* (Cambridge, Mass.: MIT Press, 1988).

16. From the nineteenth century on, these archaeological ruins became known as the Golden House of Nero. See Frances K. Barasch, *The Grotesque,* (The Hague: Mouton, 1971), 17–19.

17. [Marcus Pollionis] Vitruvius, *De Architectura,* ed. S. Ferri (Rome: Palumbo, 1960), VII, v, 3.

18. Vitruvius, *De Architectura,* VII, v, 4.

19. John D. Summers, *The Language of Michelangelo* (Princeton: Princeton University Press, 1981), 103.

20. Quoted by Summers, *Michelangelo,* 136.

21. Mikhail Bakhtin, *Rabelais and His World* (Bloomington: Indiana University Press, 1984), 26.

22. Bakhtin, *Rabelais,* 26.

23. Boccioni, *Pittura,* 403.

24. Friedrich C. Nietzsche, *Human, All-too-Human* (Lincoln: University of Nebraska Press, 1984), aphorism.

25. The idea of architectural project is still foreign to the anglophone world of architecture; see Kenneth Frampton, "The Anthropology of Construction," *Casabella,* 251–52 (1986): 12–16.

26. Maurice Merleau-Ponty, *The Visible and the Invisible* (Evanston: Northwestern University Press, 1968), 271.

27. Relazione di progetto, Roma, marzo 1911, Archivio della Camera di Commercio di Mantova, *Busta,* 473–75.

28. Jean Dubois et al., *Dizionario di Linguistica* (Bologna: Zanichelli, 1978), 208.

29. Benedetto Croce, *Aesthetic* (Boston: Nonpareil Books, 1978), 214.

30. For Baumgarten's *pulchre cogitandi* see Bernard Bosanquet, *A History of Aesthetics* (London: Allen & Unwin 1892), 182–87.

31. F. Piselli, "*Le rifessioni sul testo poetico di Alexander G. Baumgarten,*" *Aesthetica/Bina* 13 (1986): 14.

32. For the use of sarcastic and pornographic language in grotesque figures see Bakhtin, *Rabelais,* ch. 3.

33. Letter from Andreani to President Camera di Commercio Usigli, Feb. 11, 1911, Archivio della Camera di Commercio di Mantova, *Busta,* 403.

34. This villa is located in the small country town where the great poet Virgil Marone was born.

35. Edward Said, *Beginnings* (New York: Columbia University Press, 1975), 13.

36. Said, *Beginnings,* 8.

37. This writing is dedicated to Matteo Frascari (1-5-1973/3-23-1988).

Architecture and the Ruined Millionaire: A Plea for Anarchy

Grey Gowrie

Architecture is where art and society meet most poignantly. The meeting is poignant—like an intense love affair which is at once ecstatic and unhappy—because the shaping, making, achieving of art generates a profound happiness, whether you do it yourself or experience it vicariously. A child making a mud pie is happy and so is the watching parent. Buildings are different: they are not mud pies, they are not art. They are shaped by art and they affect art in their turn. They are very close to art and once in a while, when for various reasons everything goes right, they even transcend art. The old Manhattan skyline (pre-1970) from the ocean, present-day Chicago, Chartres cathedral from the north, and Durham transcend even the charge given by Velazquez, late Rembrandt or Beethoven, or Shakespeare of the late comedies. They stand right up there against the horizon of the greatest human achievements.

Yet buildings are not art. In two essentials they differ. They are social, collective things. Neither in creation nor in what happens to them after can they escape the peculiar disappointments and compromises that all collective endeavors involve. Then they are obtrusive in a way works of art are not. It is difficult to escape from buildings. You can dodge bad art, or even good art if it overwhelms you. Contrary to the pieties of most intellectual or art-minded people, myself included, you can in fact live an intelligent, useful, and fulfilled life without concerning yourself with art at all, good or bad: we can all think of such people. You cannot dodge architecture. Architecture is politics: look at that word, from the Greek word for town. Architecture is economics: look at that word, from the Greek word for household. Architecture is frozen politics and economics, as pervasive and accusing as the salt statue of Lot's wife looking back at the writhing cities of the plain. Architecture is what we live in to get away from and what we go out of to get back to.

In a recent lecture, Richard Rogers used a number of telling phrases, as one would expect of him. One was "the grammar of esthetics." Talking about his Lloyd's building he said: "The northeast tower is the largest; it marks the principal en-of working well. Kings Cross Station. Early nineteenth-century docks and warehouses. North Sea oil rigs (think what Turner would have made of them). The factories of the second industrial revolution: infotech rather than heavy industry, robots rather than people, microchips rather than turbines. The new factories reflect a cleansing and a reduction of scale. They have also found the right architectural idiom for what they are: neat, weatherized, plastic-coated sheeting over a brick or brick-clad base. The plastic clapboard allows a welcome return of bright colors to architecture. Administrative architecture, the office block, is way behind: perhaps because the function of offices is itself beginning to change; perhaps because of the feast and famine caused by economic cycles, speculation, and overcapacity. Let me single out, as correctives, three goods *neos:* the Government Offices at Richmond Terrace (neo-Tudor); the Richard Rogers Lloyd's Building (neo-Baroque); the Chapman and Taylor offices in Bessborough Gardens (neo-Modernist).

Lastly, the high holidays of the spirit. I was fortunate to work for nearly fifteen years in a human masterpiece: the Houses of Parliament by Barry and Pugin. Of course they, too, are *neos.* But I believe that they are the greatest neo-Gothic buildings and equal to many of the great medieval buildings that inspired them. They have scale and splendor, airiness and ability to take the light. So they trick the eye into believing that they too are light, as opposed to ponderous, buildings. They have pomp, as they are supposed to, but no pomposity. When I look at the Big Ben clock tower especially, I think of a line Sylvia Plath wrote about a baby: "You are the one solid the spaces lean on, envious."

The parliament building is an icon for Parliament's own supremacy. As one subject to the Queen in Parliament, I do not want M. Delors to take that away from me. It amused me that when the French did us the honor of the great Turner exhibition at the Louvre a few years ago, they chose his picture of the burning of the old Houses of Parliament for the poster. It is probably the building most people outside this country would identify with us. I do not think it is as great as Durham; I do think it as great as St. Paul's.

Even if you ignore the iconographic significance of the building, you have to recognize its extraordinary architectural sensitivity to the Thames valley light. Consider Monet's great series of paintings of this building. He understood about light. And Richard Seifert, whom I happen to believe is a very fine architect indeed (Centre Point, the Royal Kensington Hotel, the decent NatWest tower, which I should perhaps have included under functionalism) once declared that you need broken surfaces, not concrete slabs, to take the London light. I certainly agree, and my own favorite post-war building in London is the Post Office Tower — another icon of its age and function but also very sensitive to its locale. (And also sexy, and also fun.)

We are eclectic beings, creatures of moods. A culture and an architecture will reflect different moods if left to themselves. Uniformity is the product of a governing esthetic. If you scratch a governing esthetic, you will usually uncover a government of some kind. Liberal democracy is by definition pluralist. Its architecture is liable to reflect this. Don't forget that the wide boulevardes with which Napoleon III replaced the medieval streets of Paris had a lot to do with moving troops about quickly and keeping public order.

Of course I acknowledge that on the road to greater freedom we shall have to pass some pretty horrible buildings. But the ugliness is not usually a product of the freedom. Often it derives from the imposition of some kind of constraint. There will always be constraints; the challenge of liberal democracy is getting rid of the unnecessary ones. Bad government produces the kind of thinking that produces bad buildings. Big aggregations of capital tend to do the same. The Shell Building on the South Bank looks like the Pentagon.

So the core of my argument is that we should make a virtue out of the tendency, endemic in a liberal as contrasted with a social democracy, towards stylistic disorder and eclectic diversity. If we do so we shall soon forge from it a distinctive style of our own; I see signs of this in Tokyo, one of my favorite cities. I believe that if we could only learn to trust liberty and wade a little deeper into its waters, we would be rewarded by "new styles of architecture, a change of heart," in Auden's phrase. These might not aim for permanence (liberalism generates a rapid turnover of ideas and uses). They would make up for it by the gaiety and inventiveness with which they responded to the inevitable physical, environmental, and political constraints. If people vote for a green belt, for example, its imposition requires zoning and planning ingenuity on the part of the authorities in respect of the space that remains. This leads to ingenuity on the part of the architects, at least if they are to be responsive to the psychological as well as the physical requirements of human beings.

Personally, I am in favor of linear rather than concentric development. If London stretched to Bristol along the M4, to the Chiltern ridge along the M40, and to Basingstoke along the M3, we would have all the space required for economic growth for another century at least. The green belt could start as little as a mile in (less in many places) from either side of these lines of communication. Existing dormitory villages would be protected; some of the less than wonderful developments of recent years could, if we wished, be greened over in time.

If you have followed me so far, you will see that the grammar of esthetics is really only a phrase for the grammar of perception; and the grammar of perception is the breaking down we do—the deconstruction, to use a fashionable phrase—in order to arrive at the psychology of perception. To some degree this will be relative, depending on where we stand in relation to space and time (move, I suppose, would be a more accurate word than stand). Satirists have much to teach us about the relativity of perceptions. The curves of the female body have been emblems of beauty in western art, at least since the seventeenth century. Yet you will remember that in Gulliver's Travels, in the Brobdignag section, the breast and nipple of Gulliver's nurse is so gigantic, so anatomically revealing, that the relatively Lilliputian-sized Gulliver is revolted. Then again you will remember Bunuel's film *The Discreet Charm of the Bourgeoisie*. Communal defecation is the polite social norm. Eating is a necessary but improper function, to be undertaken in a small locked room only and in private.

Scale and angle have a lot to do with the harmonics of architecture as well as with perception. But architecture is also normative, by which I mean that the built environment constitutes a fixed empirical mark for our perceptions, a magnetic pole for our sense of the world and our place in it. This is the bit where the grammar of perception feeds back into esthetics and gets involved with things looking good and with ourselves feeling good and behaving better. However jumbled in esthetic and historical terms—perhaps *because* jumbled in esthetic and historical terms, perhaps because of its very relativity—architecture is a determinant of happiness. Happiness is better, as Mae West said of being rich. And we have some grounds for believing that happy people behave better than unhappy ones, towards themselves and others; not necessarily well, but better. This is where we come to the remaining sides of the building, the social and economic sides.

Everyone here knows Wordsworth's poem "Composed upon Westminster Bridge." It is a poem so shot through with happiness it seems only a kindness, since it is short, to recite it.

> Earth has not anything to show more fair:
> Dull would he be of soul who could pass by
> A sight so touching in its majesty:
> This City now doth, like a garment, wear
> The beauty of the morning; silent, bare,
> Ships, towers, domes, theatres and temples lie
> Open unto the fields, and to the sky;
> All bright and glittering in the smokeless air.
> Never did sun more beautifully steep
> In his first splendour, valley, rock, or hill;
> Ne'er saw I, never felt, a calm so deep!
> The river glideth at his own sweet will:
> Dear God! the very houses seem asleep;
> And all that mighty heart is lying still!

Following Wordsworth, you could say that architecture gives us an image of a mighty heart. It realizes collective purpose, the visible sense that even if we feel lonely and unhappy we are not in fact alone; that even when we acknowledge that we are temporary beings and face the fact of our extinction, we feel that architecture will still be there, for a few years or centuries longer. So good architecture is important: to happiness, to morality.

If you agree, the converse is also likely to be the case. Bad architecture hurts. One of the reasons for the rather common perception that Britain is not a very happy society today has to do with architecture. Very many people feel bad about our architecture, about our built environment. Architects have in recent years felt themselves to be under attack professionally or at best unappreciated and misunderstood. I am not just referring to the Prince of Wales affair, although that was important, a watershed. HRH, who is a formidable communicator, focused, not least for the mass media and therefore the general public, upon a discontent that had been pervasive for at least twenty years. Its sharp end had to do with the living conditions of poor people and some ethnic minorities in cities and with people's actual and perceived relation to violent crime in cities. I also want to underline the phrase I just used about *the perception* that Britain is not a very happy society today. The perception certainly exists. It is an a priori in much of the debate about architecture. I am concerned with the psychology of the perception, and its relation to architecture, not whether it is valid, or whether there is such a thing as a happy society. I suspect there is not, at least where advanced societies are concerned. I suspect that happiness is an individual, not a collective, matter. But as I have said, I also believe that our social morality, and therefore our collective behavior, is at least improved by as many individuals experiencing as many moments of happiness as possible.

Let me sketch the configuration of the debate very quickly. In the corner of public discontent, the Prince's corner so to say, there is the sense that architects, planners, and local and national politicians are insensitive to the needs of the community; that they plan and build structures they would not live in themselves if they could afford not to and they *can* afford not to; that the structures are impractical, ugly, sometimes unsafe, difficult to protect or police; that in aggregate they constitute environments that encourage rather than deter crime and violence; that the idea and actuality of neighborhood and neighborliness have been subsumed by statistical aggregates and economic imperatives. In the corner of professional discontent (let us call it Maxwell Hutchinson's corner for he it was who answered the Prince, and very well, in his book *The Prince of Wales: Right or Wrong? An Architect Replies*), there is the sense that architects' briefs are wholly cost determined and that central government controls over local spending mean that the pace of correcting previous errors has slowed down. (It was, after all, central and local government, acting under a consensus of opinion in both major political parties, which in the 1950s and 1960s led to the setting of fast and furious housing and rehousing targets. There was massive public support for the policy at the time.) There is also a sense among architects that the media furor initiated by Prince Charles's original speech — and by the causes he has subsequently championed (Rod Hackney, Leon Krier, pitched roofs) — did deafen all ears to accounts of the very real way in which the problems he identified were 1950s and 1960s problems already in the process of being addressed. Hutchinson does see architects working with local committees not only on the esthetics of the built environment but also on its logistics: getting grants for improvements, monitoring environmental and safety standards, and doing all this on a fee-contingency basis only.

I understand the passions generated by these arguments and on the whole side with the architects. As I suggested at the beginning, architecture is frozen politics and economics; it is these we need to address. These social issues are not fundamentally to do with the grammar of esthetics or the grammar of perception. But of course they do also affect how things look: the look is liable to come right when the socioeconomic needs are fulfilled, or at least improved. To be blunt, community architecture issues and dissatisfaction have a lot to do with poverty. We do not use the word community very often in connection with well-off people. There is little fuss over the Mayfair, or Purley, or Chester, or Edinburgh New Town communities.

My own political views on the amelioration of poverty are relevant to this talk only where they touch on architecture. Very broadly, I believe that in the main it is better for people on low incomes to have income support, to have money, which they then use to purchase competitive services, than for them to depend on free provision of the services themselves. The word "free" must come in quotes because of course it is the people on lowish, if not very low incomes, who are paying for them through tax. The sensible thing is to transfer as much tax revenue as possible in cash to people on low incomes. I find it offensive and patronizing — a variant of the Victorian coals in the bath argument — to suggest that people who are not very well off cannot in the vast majority of cases supply their needs themselves by employing cash. They do not need to sustain state monopolies supposed to help them and sustain them at relatively high levels of job security and pay. If this seems unduly contentious, please refer to Maxwell Hutchinson, who I would not have thought had a Thatcherite bone in his body, when he tells us how the community architect has to spend most of his time hassling with the caring classes: people who are quite well paid to look after people who are not.

The serious and adverse effect on architecture of these political and economic issues is encapsulated in the first bit of the rather cryptic title of my talk: "Architecture and the Ruined Millionaire." It comes, as I am sure you will have recognized, from T. S. Eliot's wartime poem "East Coker."

The whole earth is our hospital
Endowed by the ruined millionaire,
Wherein, if we do well, we shall
Die of the absolute paternal care
That will not leave us but prevents us everywhere.

Eliot's lines, written in time of not only war but the Beveridge Report and the
Butler Education Act, seem to me to be a wonderful apostrophe of the Welfare
State. Like all good poetry, you can take them literally or figuratively, in or out of
context. It is, for instance, a grim and literal thought that in Britain our grandest,
in the sense of largest, buildings over the past twenty or thirty years have been
offices of administration and hospitals. St. Thomas's white-tiled clinicism faces
Barry and Pugin's and perhaps London's masterpiece: the Houses of Parliament.
Farther down the Thames from St. Thomas's is Guy's Hospital, which is my can-
didate for the ugliest building in London. A cross between an up-ended industrial spanner and some awful building out of Kafka—the real headquarters of the
KGB is a poetic enclosure by comparison—Guy's profile wrecks Tower Bridge
from everywhere but the south and dominates much of the interesting Dockland
revival as well. I am sure that Guy's is a great hospital, with a dedicated staff. But
if you had to enter, it, wouldn't your morale sink even lower? Bad architecture is
morally bad; it causes harm. At best, if that is too cruel, it constitutes an emblem
of harm. Another sumptuous poet, Philip Larkin, writing thirty years after Eliot,
called his poem about a hospital, significantly, "The Building." It is too long to
read in full but here are the beginning and the end, appropriately enough for
hospitals.

Higher than the handsomest hotel
The lucent comb shows up for miles, but see,
All round it close-ribbed streets rise and fall
Like a great sigh out of the last century.
The porters are scruffy; what keep drawing up
At the entrance are not taxis; and in the hall
As well as creepers hangs a frightening smell.

There are paperbacks, and tea at so much a cup,
Like an airport lounge, but those who tamely sit
On rows of steel chairs turning the ripped mags
Haven't come far. More like a local bus,
These outdoor clothes and half-filled shopping bags
And faces restless and resigned, although
Every few minutes comes a kind of nurse

To fetch someone away: the rest refit
Cups back to saucers, cough, or glance below

I part company with Richard Rogers in his assumption that culture is subordinating public values to private greed. The reverse, if anything, is the case. The public values we have—I am thinking of health and some, not all, of the social benefits—are simply outstripping the productive side of our economy. This is true whichever political party is in government. It is a concern shared, I can tell you from experience, by the governments of Sweden, Germany, and Spain; I do not know about France. And the margarine is being thinly spread. There may be nothing wrong with the welfare state but it was *not* designed by the wartime coalition government or implemented by the postwar Labour government to service a relatively affluent bourgeoisie.

Transferring cash rather than paying for the provision of services is one way out of the dilemma. It is a partial remedy. All remedies, in a democracy, should perhaps be partial: at the margin, step-by-step. I do not know when either of our political parties will make a start: oddly enough Labour under Denis Healey and Joel Bennett at the Treasury in 1977–78 did so, only to resile when the International Monetary Fund went away. Ted Heath's administration introduced improvement grants. It was and is cheaper and more desirable for people to refurbish and improve their homes and neighborhoods themselves than to find themselves housed and serviced according to some enlightened specification which turns out to be the prevailing wisdom and fashion of a given generation of architects and city planners and local officials. The present administration is wrestling with the difficulties of bringing local government expenditure under control at the same time as making it more accountable. If this seems a contradiction in terms, remember that 70 percent of local government expenditure comes as grant-in-aid from central government. He (or rather she) who pays 70 percent of the piper should at least be able to call some of the tunes. Be this as it may, I do know that it is useless to look to the public sector for *significant* direct patronage in architecture or the arts until public expenditure is down as a proportion of Gross Domestic Product. The unfulfillable expectations of social democracy threaten liberal democracy. This is bad in a number of ways and very bad for architecture. The ruined millionaire has too many calls on his purse; the error of life itself costs too much money to put right.

This being the case, it seems unlikely that we shall in the next thirty years or so (it is foolish to look further than one generation) undertake the kind of comprehensive developments in most of our major cities, in London especially, which Christopher Wren failed to achieve after the fire and which John Nash and Thomas Cubitt to a considerable extent did achieve, under free enterprise, in Regent's Park and Belgravia respectively. I should perhaps cite an exception in the form of the Canary Wharf redevelopment. I have to confess that this project looks a bit Ceaucescuian to me. I am also doubtbul about the supply-demand equation in relation to offices.

While the desire to preserve harmony in marriages will no doubt continue to ensure that one or both partners in a marriage leave home during the day, it is odd that we are building so many more offices at the very moment in history when technology allows us to conduct cottage industries on a global scale. A significant minority of those who commute into London from the suburbs or beyond could even now, I suggest, work out of home or in some corporate building a few minutes from their home: a faxed, satellited, on-line village hall. Computers can put an end to commuters.

When I look at the Shell Building on the South Bank I see a monument less to corporate greed, in Rogers's terms, than to the administrative and managerial habits of the 1950s and 1960s. It is a dire structure, a respectable runner-up to Guy's Hospital in awfulness. Bunching hundreds of little offices beside and on top of each other suggests a totalitarian way of doing things, or at least an over-hierarchical one. That is why the architecture has Mussolinian (without the Italian flair) and Brezhnevian associations: I was going to say Stalinesque but his terrifying bureaucratic gulags do also retain some of *his* manic flair. (Squint and you see a cathedral.) The social equivalent of these kinds of buildings are the great residential tower blocks or cliffs (like one in Sheffield) which more than anything gave architects a bad name but which had been rejected by both society and the profession well before the Prince of Wales gave his speech. To get back to my theme, given that it is unlikely that we shall do a Napoleon III or a Haussman and develop significant portions of our capital or any of our other cities comprehensively, why not make a virtue of building with the grain of our history and national character, only better than we have managed in recent years.

This is where the second phrase of the title comes in, the plea for anarchy. London is an anarchic city, a collection of towns and villages. Things have gone wrong when social or commercial policy or the perennial transport wrangles have ensured developments which are against the grain of our city. If on a clear day you fly in from north or west, loop round Hertfordshire, and follow the Thames down to Heathrow, you will see that whereas English agriculture gives the countryside a planned, efficient, increasingly soul-less appearance, London looks to your Brobdignagian eye like a medieval landscape: here open strip, there common land, garden enclosure here, there wilderness: all together, higgledy-piggledy. A few imperatives reveal themselves. One is that South London needs a park, a decent-sized one, between Greenwich and Richmond. The other is that it would be sensible in practical terms and also esthetically satisfying (perhaps I should say and *therefore* esthetically satisfying) for Heathrow to lie within a city rather than a suburb.

It is sensible to place commercial developments around and along the principal lines of transport and communication. Offices, factories, and warehouses do not make a fuss about an extra runway here and there in the way residents, understandably, are prone to do. Low-rise commercial development beside the major motorways (the M4 provides a recent example) actually serves to *protect* green-belt villages from visual and environmental pollution. An added advantage is that people can live and raise children in quasi-rural surroundings, which is what many people want, without traveling very far. And green-minded people should remember that not traveling very far is a sensible way of reducing atmospheric pollution, be it the product of automobile emissions or electricity generation.

If you were flying in a light aircraft rather than a jumbo-jet, you could also spot another imperative: indeed you can do so from the ground. The Thames is wasted. It needs trees and grass and pleasant apartment buildings and houses and a compatible mix of institutions. A model might be the Charles River between Boston and Cambridge in Massachusetts, only on a much larger scale. All this is achievable. We could start right away. London could give itself a splendid millennial birthday present. It is not even expensive, because all it requires is a legislative framework of zoning, with some flexibility built into it. The framework allows for so much residential, so much commercial, so much industrial, and so much open space. Over time, the market does the rest. But the achievable Utopia (or significant improvement, at least) needs a political revolution: a strong central authority prepared to use its muscle in respect of structure and communications only and be hands off, liberal, in respect of everything else. If you lean to the left, it could be a reconstituted Greater London Council. If you lean to the right, it could be the Secretary of State for the Environment backed by the Prime Minister and the Cabinet. If, like me, you are a dinosaur, a free-market Gladstonian liberal, you could swallow your principles and go with one or the other. I would go with the right because I see no signs that local government in Britain will ever sufficiently attract men and women of caliber. "Ever" is an overstatement; let us say in the next generation. The attraction of the House of Commons is too strong and perhaps in a small country we should not be surprised at this.

I want to end where I began, with the psychology of perception. You will have noticed that much of what I have had to say has been concerned with sociology or politics or economics. It is tempting to avoid them and concentrate on the look of buildings, the esthetics. We cannot do so because architecture is where art and society meet. But if the human predilection for untidiness, for not submitting ourselves for very long to a formalized or methodical way of doing things (within the species this is also a very British characteristic), if freedom itself is to generate good buildings and sympathetic city scapes and the consequent amelioration of the wrong kinds of anarchy—violence and alienation—if we are, in Empson's phrase, to learn a style from a despair, then our architecture needs to be psychologically intelligent, responsive not just to human needs but to human contradictions as well.

mplex and contradictory.] [All too readily, more] "is a bore."

chitectural production and architectural discourse of the last
devolved from what was more a mood than a thesis, a mood
ant of a debased modernism. Too often, both modernism and
problems they still present even in their most convincing
e not been confronted directly. Architecture has turned in on
a limited vision of itself.

nd" architecture. There may be many ways to give substance
grounding, but we may start with a few recognitions.
production is political. The position of architecture within
the remarkable world political events of today demands attention, even as it
must also be seen within the current inane political condition of America.

○ Architecture belongs to our physical and cultural environment, and must
define its position within the most comprehensive understanding of that environment. No artifact is static; every maker and interpreter continuously
adds to our potentials, altering the context and the significance of what has
been received.

○ Architecture is material. At present not only the remarkably adaptive ca-
pacities of ever greater ranges of materials and production, but also the
alienated state of architectural discourse discourage attention to its material
base. We must reinvigorate the knowledge of making.

Attention to architecture as politics, as physical and cultural environment, and as
materiality are three of no doubt many ways to move out of the seductive but finally arid autonomy or architecture. Yet this call to reclaim and extend the ground
of architecture is only half the story.

There is an architecture still. The discipline of architecture has its own cognitive
base: its problems, theories, and methods, which are not reducible to other bodies
of knowledge.[1] There are reciprocities between the discipline of architecture and

the physical and cultural context of its realization; yet it is precisely in these reciprocities that one can identify what is unique to architecture, what I would call the quasi-autonomy of the architectural discipline. It is this quasi-autonomy which the vehicles of architectural education and research, including its journals and publications, must identify, challenge, and nurture.

By the "discipline of architecture" I understand a collective body of knowledge that is unique to architecture and which, growing over time, is not delimited in time or space. Trabeated structural systems and wall and vault construction may be studies in purely technical terms, and this is necessary to architecture. When, however, such systems are understood to create opportunities and constraints for the definition of space, the ordering of circulation, and the play of light, these are issues of the discipline of architecture. Le Corbusier's "Five Points" were a contribution to the discipline which relied upon, but were not determined by, new structural potentials. To distinguish the surface of a wall from the wall itself, and to find in this distinction the opportunity for representation is a proposition within the discipline of architecture. The structure of knowledge within the discipline is such as to preserve the memory and continue the study of that which is external to the range of current practice. Similarly, it is from a base within the discipline that one can speculate and project what might be, unconstrained by the need to synthesize a solution within the time frame of a client. Thus there is a distinction between the products of the profession and the discipline of architecture. The physical artifact, the building, the product of the profession, absolutely requires a synthesis whether well or badly performed. The products of the discipline take many forms and possess their own integrity, but emphasize a given aspect of architecture or an expansive theoretical synthesis; the discipline establishes resources for architectural production rather than taking that final step towards closure.

Oscillation between expansiveness and focus is congruent with what I understand as a non-elitist "discipline of architecture." The discipline derives focus and boundaries from what is unique in its concern with people and their environments. The discipline is expansive in that the content of this discipline is not the privilege of a few professionals, nor is it bounded by the concerns of the current moment. The craftsman, the builder, the engineer; the entrepreneur, gardener, preservationist, and historian; as well as many other specialists, and indeed the amateur, and every citizen will be at times concerned with, and a potential contributor to, the discipline of architecture. Some of these concerns and potentials may be anachronistic relative to current architectural practice, and may seem overly pragmatic, antiquated, or utopian; yet they are properly within the discourse of the discipline.

I would pose as the challenge of a new publication in architecture that it encourage both expansiveness and focus. At this moment, it must induce critical debate over the reintegration of the cultural and material ground of architecture, while it maintains the recognition of that which is unique to the discipline of architecture. Such a dialog will reaffirm that the cultural realm of the discipline of architecture is never coincident with the material realm; rather, the discourse will examine in full consciousness the opening or closing of that gap, and its articulation. In that awareness and that task reside both the responsibility and the glory of a non-elitist and socially engaged discipline called architecture.

Note

1. This essay was developed from the notes for a presentation at the University of Michigan in 1988, entitled "The Discipline of Architecture."

Constancy and Change in Architecture was composed into type on a Compugraphic digital phototypesetter in eleven point Sabon with two points of spacing between the lines. Sabon was also selected for display. The book was designed by Cameron Poulter, typeset by Metricomp, Inc., printed offset by Hart Graphics, Inc., and bound by Custom Bookbinders, Inc. The paper on which this book is printed carries acid-free characteristics for an effective life of at least three hundred years.

TEXAS A&M UNIVERSITY PRESS : COLLEGE STATION